THE HUMANITIES IN INDIA AS PLURALIST PEDAGOGY

Studies in Comparative Literature
Jadavpur University

Studies in Comparative Literature, Jadavpur University, is founded on the view that the study of literatures and the arts in multilingual and culturally diverse contexts such as India demands a comparative approach. It is informed by an interdisciplinary and intercultural focus on bhasha literatures, translation, orality and performance as well as other arts and digital humanities, in the context of local, national and international literary and cultural transactions. The series is meant for students, scholars, and teachers of comparative literature as well as of single literature and other humanities departments. It brings together the work of faculty members and scholars at the Department of Comparative Literature, Jadavpur University, as well as of national and international visiting scholars who have enriched its research and debates.

Sub-series I: Texts, Contexts, Methods

Ia. Histories and Paradigms
Ib. Approaching New Challenges, Recasting Paradigms

Sub-series II: Indian and Asian Contexts

Sub-series III: Literature and Other Knowledge Systems

IIIa. Literary Studies and Performance
IIIb. Literature and Indigenous Knowledge Systems

Sub-series IV: Lecture Series

Contributions based on talks by Visiting Scholars

STUDIES IN COMPARATIVE LITERATURE
JADAVPUR UNIVERSITY

SUB-SERIES IV: LECTURES

THE HUMANITIES IN INDIA AS PLURALIST PEDAGOGY

Daniel J. Rycroft
Chair, India Dialogue
University of East Anglia (UK)

Orient BlackSwan

THE HUMANITIES IN INDIA AS PLURALIST PEDAGOGY

ORIENT BLACKSWAN PRIVATE LIMITED

Registered Office
3-6-752 Himayatnagar, Hyderabad 500 029, Telangana, India
E-mail: centraloffice@orientblackswan.com

Other Offices
Bengaluru, Chennai, Guwahati, Hyderabad, Kolkata,
Mumbai, New Delhi, Noida, Patna, Visakhapatnam

First published 2023

ISBN 978-93-5442-731-2

Typeset in Adobe Garamond Pro 12.5/15.6 *by*
Shine Graphics, Delhi 110 094

037687

Printed at
Thomson Press, New Delhi 110020

Published by
Orient Blackswan Private Limited
3-6-752, Himayatnagar, Hyderabad 500 029, Telangana, India
E-mail: info@orientblackswan.com

Contents

General Introduction *vii*

The Humanities in India as Pluralist Pedagogy 1

References 86

General Introduction

The first full-fledged department of Comparative Literature in India, and the second in Asia, was established in Calcutta at Jadavpur University in 1956. The reputed Bangla poet, writer and scholar Buddhadeva Bose was its founder and the first Head of the Department. The *Jadavpur Journal of Comparative Literature*, launched here in 1961, is one of the oldest journals in Asia that has continued, regularly, to publish significant research in comparative literature by national and international scholars. In the late 1980s the UGC earmarked the department for promotion of teaching and research under its Special Assistance Programme. In the early nineties the department widened its areas of interest to first introduce courses in the literatures and cultures of Bangladesh, Africa, Canada and Latin America; then it set up centres in the latter three, subsequently a Centre for Translation of Indian Literatures, and, most recently, a Centre for Studies of Islamicate Asia. During the Tenth Plan the department was also selected by the UGC to participate in its ASIHSS (Assistance for Strengthening of Infrastructure for Humanities and Social Sciences) programme. In addition to these UGC programmes and these centres, the UPE—University with Potential for Excellence—programme of the UGC also enabled the establishment of research projects in the department. These included translation and intercultural studies under Project Anuvad; documentation and research relating to performers of traditional dramatic forms in different districts of West Bengal under Project Palagaan; and a unique new venture involving an exploration of Kolkata through narratives of sound under the project Soundscapes. The first and so far only UGC Centre of Advanced Study in Comparative Literature in India was also established in this department in 2005, and it continued promoting research into its third phase. This series, Studies in Comparative Literature, Jadavpur University, is rooted in this academic history of over six decades.

When other departments of Comparative Literature finally began to be established in India in the 1990s, a sharing of our research and pedagogic experience became imperative. As the practice of comparative literature proliferated in centres and newly established departments as well as in single literature departments right across India, we began to face persistent requests for enhanced access to our research from academics, researchers and students alike. Our research, while considerable, had largely been published by local presses and the university, and did not have the national outreach now demanded of it. It was in response to this need that the idea of initiating a series with a reputed mainstream national publisher came about, and we are especially happy about this partnership with Orient BlackSwan, given the important role it has played in the dissemination of scholarship on Indian literatures and cultures.

We hold that the study of literatures and the arts in multilingual and culturally diverse countries such as ours demands a comparative approach; hence, Studies in Comparative Literature, Jadavpur University, is a series for students, scholars and teachers of comparative literature as well as of single literature, arts and other humanities departments. It explores a range of histories, theoretical reflections, as well as innovative approaches and concerns relevant to the field of comparative literature. In keeping with the basic imperatives of comparative literature, it is both intercultural and interdisciplinary in that it engages with the trajectories of literatures across cultures as well as with the relations between literatures and other fields of creative expression. It is thus informed by an interdisciplinary and intercultural focus on *bhasha* literatures, translation, orality and performance as well as other arts and digital humanities, in the context of local, national and international literary and cultural transactions, and also those of the borderlands.

This series brings together the work of faculty and scholars at the department of Comparative Literature, Jadavpur University, and of national and international visiting scholars. It comprises both edited volumes and authored books, as well as monographs by visiting scholars. The series launches the research carried out under the third phase of the UGC Centre of Advanced Study in Comparative Literature, and the publication of these volumes, we hope, will mark the beginnings of a renewed mapping of comparative literary studies in India.

The current studies build on the foundations of creative intellectual vision, innovative pedagogy and several decades of original scholarship that went into the shaping of what was a new field of study, in fact a new mode of inquiry, in the Indian university. Many generations have enriched comparative literary studies in India, and it is impossible to chart all the contributions of even just those at the Department of Comparative Literature at Jadavpur University in the space of a short introduction such as this. What follows however is a brief account of the directions of research, and of the kinds of publications that emerged from this research, as well as in response to pedagogic needs at this department; it is being presented here as an academic contextualisation for the present series that may be useful to other scholars, centres and departments of not just comparative literature but also literary studies in general.

Before mapping the broad areas of research across the decades however, it may be relevant to reflect for a moment on the intellectual and creative range of teachers and scholars who contributed to its making. Buddhadeva Bose and Sudhindranath Dutta were towering modern Bangla poets and writers, and amongst the foremost intellectuals of their time. Joining them in the early years were Fr. Robert Antoine, a Belgian Jesuit priest who was a Sanskritist and a scholar of Greek and Latin, who translated Kalidasa's *Raghuvamsa* from the Sanskrit into English, and also collaborated on a translation of Virgil's *Aeneid* from the Latin into Bangla; Fr. Pierre Fallon, who was also a Belgian Jesuit priest, a professor of French literature, a licenciate in philosophy and theology and an expert in Bangla philology; and David J. McCutchion who had trained in French and German at Jesus College Cambridge, and later became an authority on both the terracotta temples as well as the *patua*s (scroll painters) of Bengal. The next two generations of teacher-scholars, five of whom also trained in M.A. or Ph.D. programmes of North American departments of Comparative Literature and others in France or Germany, included Naresh Guha, Amiya Dev, Deepak Mazumdar, Subir Roychowdhury, Swapan Mazumdar, Bijoya Das, Subha Chakraborty Dasgupta, Ipsita Chanda, Suman Ghosh, Alokeranjan Dasgupta, Pranabendu Dasgupta, Manabendra Bandyopadhyay, Nabaneeta Dev Sen, Sibaji Bandyopadhyay and Debiprasad Bhattacharya. All of them earned international repute as scholars, and while the last was a polyglot and a renowned Sanskritist, the penultimate five were also major creative writers in Bangla.

It is perhaps the wide range of exposure and training, which was as rigorous as it may seem eclectic, that cautioned scholars of this department about strait-jacketing comparative literary studies into any definitive 'school' or methodology, or of limiting Indian literary studies within the political borders of the Indian nation state. So, even in their pioneering role, they refrained from formulating a Jadavpur 'school' of Comparative Literature, or privileging any comparative methodology over others. They also desisted from confining literary studies to inter-Indian literary relations only, and conscientiously trained their lenses on the wider South-Asian and Asian, Perso-Arabic and Anglo-European fields too; and eventually they reached out to Latin America, Africa and Australia, especially in relation to transactions with Indian literatures and cultures, but also otherwise. Such catholicity, in both approach and range, would naturally give rise to questions of delimitation and focus—and what emerges clearly as a connecting thread across the decades is that, in terms of both literary-cultural focus and methodological approach, scholars here responded to the ground realities and the needs of their times.

It was in the early 1990s that the consolidated programme of publishing started, supported by the Special Assistance Programme of the UGC; the focus in this decade was clearly on creating resources for research. Bibliographies of reception—of World Literature in Bangla periodicals, and of Bangla literature in South Indian languages—formed one thrust area. Translation became a focal point from the beginning: translation of material such as literary manifestoes in Indian languages, and discussions regarding the aesthetics as well as comparative literature methodologies of translation featured in this phase. Literary historiography in India featured as an important concern as did East–West literary interactions of the colonial period. The fourth area of concern was in relation to third-world contexts—to cultures of silence as well as the challenge of envisioning their futures—and this included reflection on African and Latin American literatures and cultures.

The focus on generating resources for comparative research continued through the next five years with translations across several genres (poetry, short stories, plays and excerpts of autobiographies) and several languages (that is, from Bangla into other languages such as Asamiya and English, and from Odia, Gujarati, Marathi and other Indian languages into English as well as Bangla). Also, the first phase had documented debates on comparative literary approaches to historiography; this one brought into focus issues of genology from a comparative perspective, with a volume tracing the *charit* as a genre. A third area of engagement was that of linguistic and cultural formations of self-identity across the literatures of Bengal and Bangladesh, thus bringing the literature of Bangladesh into the purview of our research. This phase was also marked by the publication of three volumes under the rubric of Literary Studies in India: on Literary Historiography, Thematology and Genology; it brought together reflections of comparative literature academics as well as scholars from other literature and humanities departments, on approaches to literary studies in India at the beginning of the twenty-first century.

In the first phase of the Centre of Advanced Study (2005–2010), we continued, on the one hand with the task of generating resources for research, such as the annotated bibliography of Bangla and Asamiya histories of literature;

on the other hand we extended the work on historiography to specific areas of study such as Indian English literature. Two new sets of concerns came into focus in this period. One set related to the need to document and study the fast-disappearing body of folk performances—the outcomes included the recordings and studies of *Manasamangal pala* and *Banabibir pala*. The other set of concerns was underlined by the realisation that most of our international focus had been on literary relations with the Anglo-European world, while those with other Asian cultures had not received the attention they deserved; thus the imperative to retrieve and explore these resulted in a focus on travel literature from Asia with focus on the collection of literary material along sea and trade routes, and the publication of a bibliography of travelogues to Asian countries in Bangla as well as an anthology of Bangla and Odia writings on colonial Burma. During this phase the additional support from the Assistance for Strengthening of Infrastructure for Humanities and Social Sciences (ASIHSS) programme of the UGC enabled research in South Asian contexts and resulted in the publication of a South Asian nationalisms reader, as well as a volume on the poetics and politics of Sufism and Bhakti in South Asia.

The following years, in the second phase of the CAS, were marked by more extensive and deeperresearch in the fields already marked out. At least three areas that had clearly emerged as thrust areas were:

- Comparative Literature: Explorations in Discipline and Methodology
- Roots and Routes: Intra-Indian and Intra-Asian Linguistic, Literary and Cultural Relations
- Literature and Other Knowledge Systems

Resources generated for research during this period included a handbook on terms and concepts in comparative literature, a volume on comparative literature in Germany, and textbooks on Indian Nepali literature in English and Bangla. The publications on comparative explorations in genre included a study of the *namah*. Research on folk cultures as knowledge systems resulted in publications on *charak* and *gajan* in Bengal, another on Karbi oral traditions in the Northeast, as well as a volume on literatures and oratures as knowledge systems, based on texts from Northeast India. A comparative study on the *ghumantoo* roadies, or wanderers, of India and Canada added to this set. In the context of Asian studies, research was published on tales of medieval China. The research on South Asia extended itself to comparative studies of the literatures and cultures of borders in South Asia and the Americas; this last volume marked entry into a new area of research—Comparative Border Studies.

The present series has been envisioned as follows:

Studies in Comparative Literature, Jadavpur University

Sub-series I: Texts, Contexts, Methods

1a. Histories and Paradigms
1b. Approaching New Challenges, Recasting Paradigms

Sub-series II: Indian and Asian Contexts

Sub-series III: Literature and Other Knowledge Systems

IIIa. Literary Studies and Performance
IIIb. Literature and Indigenous Knowledge Systems

Sub-series IV: Lecture Series

Contributions based on talks by Visiting Scholars

In many ways it marks a deepening and consolidation of perspectives across the earlier decades of research; in other ways it also charts new directions in comparative literary studies. The sub-series **Texts, Contexts, Methods** includes two histories in the section *Histories and Paradigms*—one of the emergence and establishment of Indian Comparative Literature, the other a disciplinary and institutional history of comparative literature in India, based on documents preserved at Jadavpur as well as gathered from across the country. Planned along with these are anthologies on texts, contexts and concepts, and on comparative literary studies in India, with contributions from scholars across the country. The section *Approaching New Challenges, Recasting Paradigms* will introduce research in new directions that responds to contemporary challenges. Comparative Literature as a discipline has historically crossed borders in terms of time and space. One of these volumes is a response to the now pervasive trans-national histories of migrants and refugees and, focussing on the Indo-Bangladesh border, it marks a shift from the prism of the 'national' to the prism of borders and frontiers, to the epistemological perspectives of 'borderlanders'; another volume charts the transformations in comparative literary studies in light of the mutual interactions between digital humanities and literary mapping in South Asia.

The sub-series **Indian and Asian Contexts** includes both intra-Indian literary translations and a mapping of linguistic, literary and cultural relations grouped under the rubric of *Roots and Routes*, as well as translations from Bangla and Urdu of fictional and discursive writings of Muslim literati in Bengal from the early twentieth century onward. Included in this sub-series are comparative studies of 'progressive' literatures, South Asian studies of transnational writers such as Ismat Chughtai, and studies of intra-Asian engagements such as Bengal's encounters with Japan in the twentieth century.

The third sub-series, **Literature and Other Knowledge Systems**, includes a volume on reflections on methodology in the translation of performance texts in the sub-section *Literary Studies and Performance*; the sub-section on *Literature and Indigenous Knowledge Systems* carries a comparative study of Karbi and Chakma narrative traditions of Northeast India, as well as another of creation songs from India, Canada, Australia and Southeast Asia.

Finally, the **Lecture Series** comprises volumes based on talks delivered by national and international visiting scholars who have enriched the research and debates of our department, and often taken us in new directions too. We are truly grateful to Alessandro Portelli, Professor Emeritus, University of Rome La Sapienza, and Tridip Suhrud, Professor and Provost, CEPT University, Ahmedabad, for their contributions on oral history and Gandhi's languages respectively, and for their generosity in permitting us to include earlier landmark essays in their volumes. We also extend our gratitude to Robert P Goldman, Professor, University of California at Berkeley, and Daniel Rycroft, Associate Professor at the University of East Anglia for having agreed to write for us on the Valmiki *Ramayana* and the humanities in India, respectively. We thank other scholars, who have collaborated in the research on some of our publications; they include Jatin Nayak, former Professor of Utkal University, Indranil Acharya, Professor at Vidyasagar University, Subha Chakraborty Dasgupta former Professor in our own department, Shraddhanjali Tamang, also a faculty member at Jadavpur University, and writer Manoranjan Byapari.

This series is the collaborative effort of all the faculty members of the Comparative Literature department: Suchorita Chattopadhyay, Kunal Chattopadhyay, Aveek Majumder, Sayantan Dasgupta, Sujit Kumar Mandal, Parthasarathi Bhaumik, Epsita Halder, Debashree Dattaray and Sumit Kumar Barua. They have been working concertedly towards its publication over the last several years; and while the individual volumes will carry their respective names as authors, editors and co-authors, it needs to be put on record that this series is finally seeing the light of day through one of the most devastating pandemics in history only because of their determined collective commitment and mutual intellectual inspiration. We are also grateful to our research fellows—who will be acknowledged individually in the respective volumes—for their selfless and cheerful support. Last but not least we extend our deep gratitude to Padmaja Anant of Orient BlackSwan for her wisdom and infinite patience—it has indeed been a pleasure working with her.

Kavita Panjabi
Samantak Das
Sucheta Bhattacharya
Series Editors

The first volumes of this series are being sent to the press with a heavy heart, for Samantak Das is with us no more. May the infallible spirit with which he contributed to the making of this series continue to enrich it in the years to come.

The Humanities in India as Pluralist Pedagogy

Introduction

This text is about the capacity of Humanities professionals to understand, teach and inspire new forms of 'academic' social responsibility. Focusing on the social significance of recent Humanities research in India, it analyses the 'patterns of values and responsibility' that emerge in contexts of educational and representational reform, such as indigenous heritage-work and institutional decolonisation (McKeon 1960, 545). It highlights the role of Humanities partnerships in critiquing and/or reproducing educational and socio-political value-systems (see Humanities in India Partnerships Programme 2017; 2018). It reaches its assessments via a combination of curriculum development and participant observation, to emphasise the potential of these approaches as 'humanistic methodologies' (Jorgensen 1989, 7). It works with and moves beyond the proposition that the Humanities are, given their imperial and post-imperial histories, as well as their inherent pluralism, 'conflicted' (see Braidotti and Gilroy 2016). It echoes longstanding calls for Humanities educators to recognise and reflect on their own 'discursive being' within an evolving global community (McKeon 1960, 550). It highlights the 'constituent elements of responsibility' that these processes have yielded in different contexts (McKeon 1959, 17). The text thereby calls into question the oftentimes hidden or intangible processes of value-creation, which comprise (a) the distributed presence of social responsibility in the Humanities, and (b) the alignment of the Humanities in India with global, humanist, and/or other widely shared principles, such as cultural pluralism (see UNESCO 1999). The text is oriented to readerships within and beyond the Humanities that are concerned with a realisation, whether via public policy or institutional and academic practice, of 'inclusiveness' and other social ethics that are intimated by these principles (Miri 2014, 70).

The text focuses on two case studies: (a) the Santal (Adivasi) rebellion of 1855–56 and its memorialisation in India, and (b) the University of East Anglia's 'Humanities in India Partnership Programme', as a constituent element of this university's India Dialogue. The Santal case study reflects my longstanding interest, as an anthropological historian, in the predicament of Adivasi (Indigenous/tribal) culture in colonial and postcolonial India. The other focus addresses more recent pedagogic collaborations and orientations. Whilst my thinking on the interconnectedness of various levels of (personal, social and universal) responsibility are inevitably inflected by 'Indian' and 'world' anthropologies (see Restreop 2018), what is at stake is a much more open-ended dialogue on the pedagogic significance of cultural and methodological pluralism. It is a dialogue that affirms McKeon's contention that the Humanities should become more conspicuously oriented to the complexity of rights that constitute our world community (McKeon 1968). As such, some far-reaching questions can be asked, such as: What are the multiplicity of values and value-systems that are invoked by 'intellectual' social responsibilities (see Ban 2010)? Mrinal Miri has eloquently captured the significance of this kind of philosophical orientation to 'higher' education at large: 'As we move up the levels of education, the required kind of attention is focused more and more on the world of ideas—

as communities of ideas, traditions of thought—and on how creative energy within a tradition may change the course of the tradition. [What kinds of] coherence and conflict exist among communities of ideas?' (Miri 2014, 20–21) Like Miri, I am largely concerned with developing a critical and self-reflexive understanding of the proposition that to be educated (in the formal sense) is to be 'educated in values' (Miri 2014, 24).

The format of the text is rather unusual in that all of the subsections are very similarly titled, in terms of 'The voices of X and Y'. As we will discover, I am not always speaking as the voice that is being represented. Rather, I am reflecting on the qualities of listening to and learning 'with' these voices. In other words, the text is a response to the provocations and values engendered by rights-oriented Humanities pedagogy and related forms of intercultural dialogue. What is addressed as 'voice' thereby refers to the symbolism and power of communication (I am with you), listening (I hear you), amplification (let them hear us), translation (they can listen with us), and reinterpretation (of voices as polyphonic) rather than to the literal or direct association of specific voices with specific people. Specific voices and specific people are involved, but they are assembled as representatives of much broader concerns. I am hoping to invoke a range of subject-positions, with a view to making the voices/provocations more 'effective' and 'multi-directional' (McKeon 1959, 400): that is to say, as workable beyond the binaries of cause and effect, and of objective and subjective knowledge. It is not that these voices have been ineffective in the past; rather that they each reappear now as part of this text's internal pluralism. The 'voices' that are involved in this dialogue are internal and external, both to me and to the various communities of academic and socio-cultural practice that I am part of. They each demand different kinds of internalisation and externalisation or, in William Desmond's terms, intermediation: 'Education is intermediation: a bringing [of ethical civility] into the commons of knowing, as well as standard forms of doing.' (Desmond 2001, 416) I am concerned with rendering the various 'voices' equal and legible and then, in different ways, mutually intelligible.

As we will see, these voices are inscribed as 'inclusion' and 'pluralism' in Part One, to ascertain some conceptual moorings; as 'responsibility' and 'provocation' in Part Two, to summon pluralist pedagogy; as the 'subject' and 'value-congruence' in Part Three, to address minority history; as 'experience' and 'transversality' in Part Four, to promote Humanities collaboration; as 'memory' and 'commemoration' in Part Five, to re-visit the Santal rebellion; as 'complexity' and 'community' in Part Six, to re-animate cultural anthropology; as 'human dignity' and 'recognition' in Part Seven, to enhance Adivasi Studies; and as 'rights' and the 'anti-colonial nation' in Part Eight, to reinterpret the pre-independence alignment of Birsa Munda and the Indian National Congress. This is an assemblage of 'voices' that speak, in different ways, with the people and issues highlighted in the two case studies. The various 'voices' that are involved and addressed in each section are sometimes co-present in other sections, even if they assume a different presence there. Throughout, I have attempted to strike a balance in emphasising both applied research, in terms of individual and collective experience, and the many pedagogical facets of cultural and methodological pluralism.

Part One: The voices of inclusion and pluralism

A pluralist approach to social responsibility embraces the proposition that various principles, philosophies, policies, practices, and pedagogies of inclusion can and should converge. These convergences have been anticipated by many intellectuals, writers, socialists, humanists, and educators in different parts of the world in recent decades, with a view to making the Humanities more fit for purpose: whether as representative of humanity and its complex constituencies, or as a conspicuously comparative, critical and intercultural response to these constituencies and their (or our) diverse social, educational, ecological, cultural and human rights (see Godrej 2009; Goodale 2018; Heskovits 2018; Thapar, et al 1970; White 2007; Wilson 1991). Keeping these kinds of rights-based agendas in full view, this text has been developed as an experiment in 'reflexive' responsibility (McKeon 1957a, 26). This is a process that was first defined by the UNESCO philosopher Richard McKeon who, as a mid-twentieth-century American internationalist and early advocate of global citizenship, sought to create a science of responsibility focusing on 'social and cultural analysis' as the prerequisite for 'higher' Humanities learning, as well as for international dialogue and diplomacy (McKeon 1957a, 5). For McKeon, 'The agent [of responsibility] may be an individual or a group acting in the context of a society or a political state, or an individual, group, or community acting in the looser association of free individuals or independent communities or states whose actions affect each other. In either situation, responsibility is a reflexive relation.' (McKeon 1957a, 26) In view of this multifaceted approach to social ethics, there are multiple ways of approaching 'reflexive' responsibility.

The different options assume different kinds of educational significance when the concept of responsibility is broached either from the perspective of the individual researcher, or else in view of group interests and identities. For example, our 'Humanities in India' steering group members (see Parts Two and Four) contributed directly to a curriculum development workshop to define 'Academic Social Responsibility', which took place at the University of Hyderabad in March 2019 (Rycroft, et al. 2020, 45–51). Whilst, of course, I agree with the findings that describe such 'intellectual' social responsibilities as (i) generating new epistemology, (ii) responding to and critiquing multilateralism, (iii) working actively against alienation (including social, economic and linguistic forms), (iv) speaking truth to power, (v) developing a new language of/for responsibility, (vi) thinking without borders, and (vii) enabling cognitive justice, it would be near impossible to work or think in accordance with all of these facets all of the time. At the level of the individual or group, therefore, a degree of ordering and re-ordering, and prioritisation and re-prioritisation, is inevitable. This kind of constant re-evaluation takes us into interesting areas of collective and transversal action and 'mind' diplomacy (see Chandramohan and Rycroft 2018): that is to say the capacity of individual thinkers to render social, political or educational the constituent elements of responsibility. Importantly, it is the institutions—such as universities, and university groupings like the Global University Network for Innovation, as well as the United Nations Academic Impact—that become the civic forums for this kind of citizen diplomacy. As a field, intellectual social responsibility therefore comes with its own 'institutional' dynamics and limitations, as noted by Miri:

> Responsibility as accountability—particularly in respect of institutions—is assessed in relation to the ends they set for themselves. ... Corporate accountability is clearly distinct from moral accountability [as they are invested in different regimes of value.] ... Universities are paradigmatic examples of institutions which aim at, promote, and are necessarily involved in [individual and group] engagement: of the kind that constitutes the core value of practice. ... There are, of course, goods to be achieved by this depending on the kind of social importance that is given to education. ... Such goods are internal to the kind of social engagement that higher education necessarily promotes. ... They may not constitute the whole of moral life, by they are necessary elements of it. ... The core accountability of the university therefore is moral accountability (2014, 40–45).

Whilst I am more interested here in exploring 'intellectual' responsibility, rather than moral accountability, Miri's argument is relevant as it helps us to appreciate the role of the university in affirming 'higher' education as an experiential and collectivised form of social practice. It is in the capacity of teachers and learners alike, to 'reassemble' the social and responsibility as interconnected domains of value, identity, or knowledge (see Latour 2005), that individual and group reflexivity will evolve. Of the aforementioned intellectual social responsibilities, I am primarily concerned with new epistemology and the development of languages, discourses and practices of social responsibility that work against alienation and exclusion.

This text explores concepts that exist 'between' global and national parameters of diversity (see Mersmann and Kippenberg 2016). Here, one is reminded of Ganesh Devy's far-sighted message concerning affirmative action policies in India, and the necessity for higher education policy to move with and 'beyond' inclusion (Devy 2013). This is an important message, as many advocates for inclusivity need to 'defy the odds' (see Singh 2013) in presenting their 'minority' rights as contiguous with inherited subject-formations, whether as Adivasi (Indigenous/tribal communities; some of which are Constituted in India as Scheduled Tribes) or Dalit (Oppressed peoples, or former Untouchables; some of which are Constituted as Scheduled Castes). This means that their/our engagement with the shifting politics and meanings of inclusion is, by necessity, in close dialogue with historical trajectories as well as the various discursive, representational and pedagogic strategies associated with these trajectories (Miri 2014, 46–75). A particular culture arises, therefore, of post-inclusion that is neither dependent nor predicated upon individual instances of inclusion as its primary measurement of success. Rather, the idea of post-inclusion moves us beyond both the numbers game, as well as the specific politics that determine the coordinates and values of this, to invoke the shifting and sometimes hidden domains through which inclusion may be experienced. It calls forth an array of cultural and social responsibilities, to invoke an important concern in studies of 'minority histories' (Chakrabarty 2004): that qualitative (and experiential) as well as quantitative (and statistical) concerns matter.

Addressing this concern, the text focuses on interpersonal and institutional experiences of 'value congruence' (see Medves 2019). As someone who self-identifies both as a Humanities pluralist and as a practitioner of specific academic fields, notably anthropological history (see Parts Six and Eight), I explore some of the practical and conceptual consequences of this interesting state of affairs. I analyse how the diverse subject-positions and subject areas that characterise the Humanities can become productive sites of value pluralism, whether in terms of their internal dynamics or else in view of their advocates' capacity to bring 'responsibility' to the surface: as a principle of higher education. For these kinds of transformation to occur, the internal and subject-specific workings of the Humanities and higher education will require more scrutiny. This demands of all practitioners a preparedness, in view of their prospective expertise in rendering the interplay of the social and responsibility integral to their work, and to their own discursive being. As noted by Joao Biehl et al: 'Once the door to the study of subjectivity is open, anthropology and its practitioners must find new ways to engage the particularities of affect, cognition, moral responsibility, and action.' (2007, 1) Approaching this list, whether as an anthropological historian or as an advocate for the 'Humanities in India', I find the prospect of these engagements timely and intriguing.

Given their capacity to summon or provoke new kinds of teaching and learning I will also explore how and why the social responsibilities of academics and universities can cohere, and then work towards the 'promotion' of social sustainability as part of a broader ethos of value pluralism (see Weber 2012). As such, I am interested in addressing the concept of 'provocative pedagogy' (Avest and Bakkar 2020), both in terms of my own and others' experiences, and in view of the potential value-congruence between Humanities research and teaching (see Fassett and Warren 2006). In brief, value pluralism alludes to the productive interplay of multiple and, indeed, competing values as and when these are brought together within, for example, fields of philosophical and educational practice. McKeon (1959) has argued that the principle of pluralism emerges as something of educational value whenever learners or thinkers get involved in different forms of communication, such as international diplomacy, philosophical dialogue, human rights activism, curriculum development, or linguistic translation. As practitioners, they are able to engage and then evaluate their own and others' subject-hood and actions within an evolving 'multiplex' of interrelated value-systems (McKeon 1964, 115). But it is Isaiah Berlin who is best known for theorising value pluralism as a concept that becomes meaningful when thinkers, educators and policy-makers broach the incommensurability that necessarily informs the 'difference' between competing values (Crowder 2019). Whenever and wherever the concept of value pluralism features within one's own thinking or decision-making, it provokes a number of questions, such as: to what extent is my own thinking reflective of different points of view, different values, or different principles? In this regard, my text explores one domain of Humanities professionalism namely value-congruence, whether this is discerned between researcher and discipline, or between higher education and society. Just as 'congruence' alludes to the idea of internal agreement, so this focus on 'academic' social responsibility prompts new questions pertaining to the role of dialogue, global subjectivity and self-reflexivity in realising these prospects.

Humanities subjectivity alludes to a 'big' question, namely the distinction between subjective and objective knowledge. Subjective knowledge pertains to the relation between experience, mind, and memory in the creation of knowledge, and to the relevance of 'knowing' to resultant behaviours and attitudes involving the self (see Kundu et al, 2009; Chambers 2013). But this text is not primarily about this distinction. Rather, it is about 'the core task of academia to provide social critique and reflection.' (Crul et al., 2020, 3) And there is an important difference too, between providing and provoking social reflection. This has been noted by Satish Deshpande in his work on inclusive higher education in India: 'The intersections of social justice and higher education are critical locations, because of their mutual implication [...] What are the implications of successful 'inclusion' for (a) the content of the learning that is imparted in higher education, and (b) its underlying values?' (Deshpande 2013, 5–6) These are far-reaching questions. Given the work that I have been involved in during the past two decades, whether as an anthropological historian or as a founder member of my university's India Dialogue initiative (see Rycroft et al, 2020; Rycroft 2021), I will aim to provide some direct responses. In sum, the text addresses the ongoing potential of the Humanities to bridge the divides between (i) the principles and values of responsibility, and (ii) diverse demands for social, ecological and institutional change.

Part Two: The voices of responsibility and provocation

In some ways, a back-to-basics approach may be required, especially when it comes to teaching and learning social responsibility. As noted by Sheldon Berman and Phyllis La Farge:

> The meaning of social responsibility is multidimensional. [...] When teachers talk about social responsibility, they first refer to it as a way of being in the world that is deeply connected to others and the environment. Being responsible goes beyond being respectful of the dignity of others. It means experiencing and appreciating our interdependence. ... It is not enough to care or to be well-informed. Social responsibility means acting on one's values, living one's values (1993, 7-8).

As a means to explore various facets of these evolving values, practices and ideals, we can productively turn to a new paradigm in the transformation of higher education, namely 'provocative pedagogy'. Through its recent articulation by Ina ter Avest and Cok Bakkar (2020), one is able to discern some key characteristics of this paradigm. These pertain to the capacity of the educator/researcher/teacher to become actively self-aware concerning (a) their own academic subjectivity, and positionality, at different points in time, and (b) the correspondence, or otherwise, between their institutional ethos and broader social, or political and cultural, value systems. They also pertain to the prospect that different facets of the overall social matrix—of economy, ecology, power, psychology, identity and difference—may be prominent or active at any given time. A core provocation, therefore, is that one needs to be alert and sensitive to the circumstantial and contextual production of educators' subject-positions, including our own, and the capacity of these circumstances and subject-positions to impart meaning and/or significance to different kinds of teaching, learning and 'developmental' interests (Peet and Hartwick 2015, 235–38).

In recent years, 'provocative pedagogy' has started to accrue some institutional traction, especially amongst educators, such as Ina ter Avest, who are involved in Dialogical Self Theory (see Meijers and Hermans 2018). The theory exists to generate for learners and teachers opportunities to nurture those facets of selfhood and educational practice that are sustained by dialogue. Given its social, moral, political and trans-disciplinary significance, the concept and practice of dialogue demands its own kind of special attention (see Freise 2018; Jezierska and Koczanowicz 2015). That said, it is broadly understood as an 'open' discourse that exists and evolves in a direct relationship with its capacity (i) to be practised across social, linguistic, geographical, institutional, religious, economic or educational divides; (ii) to summon and interweave multiple agendas, actors and 'positions'; and (iii) to address and provoke short- and long-term change. It is in these kinds of contexts that the dialogical self becomes apparent and, when this selfhood imparts something significant within education, one is drawn into the orbit of a particular phenomenon, namely dialogical learning (Muller Mirza and Dos Santos Mamed 2021). It is this phenomenon, and its capacity to generate and render significant a host of interrelations, for example between teacher and learner, self and society, and mind and experience, that informs our current evaluation of social responsibility.

Considered as the interplay (and the outcome) of overtly dialogical social practices, the potential of provocative pedagogy is significant, especially to those people, disciplines, and Higher Education Institutions which are now committed to different movements for transformation, including decolonisation (see Morreira 2020; Mignolo 2021; Wane and Todd 2018). Interestingly, a prolonged interplay of differently understood, and differently experienced, principles, provocations, and practices will need to develop if the current concern for decolonisation is to become a long-term proposition. To a large extent, it is the pluralism of the Humanities—as well as the pluralism of the methodologies that animate intercultural subject-areas like cultural and literary translation, as well as intercultural communication, museum ethnography, international relations, and many others (see Devi 1995; Elliott 2019; Phillips 2021)—that can be now brought into focus. It is via their capacity to witness, address and, in time, help to resolve the problems of colonialism and neo-colonialism that renders them socially responsible and enables social responsibility to become an active or prominent facet of both knowledge-creation and cultural production. In these open-ended terms, the prospect of provocative pedagogy is noteworthy as a means of generating new sites of individual and group consciousness that might influence or yield new self-perceptions, insights and commitments. In turn, these will evolve into their own circuits of communication and mutual understanding, and generate their own collectivised systems and expressions of value (see Vasudevan 2018).

For us, the main provocation that is articulated via dialogical pedagogy pertains to the capacity of 'higher' education or, in our case, the Humanities in India to first envisage and then facilitate more inclusive and intercultural futures for such subject areas and professions as literature, literary translation, creative writing, publishing, historiography, anthropology, museum studies, minority studies, heritage work, social ecology, environmentalism, gender equality, indigenous studies, human rights education, citizenship education, political philosophy, social movements, and social enterprise (see Das and Samaddar 2009; Vasudevan 2018). In its application, the paradigm of provocative pedagogy becomes interestingly pragmatic, especially as its advocates start to envision and then work towards the implementation of new horizons, methods and alliances (see Rycroft et al 2020, 42–44). One of our close colleagues, Prof Sayantan Dasgupta of Jadavpur University in southern Kolkata, is a true pioneer in the practice of educational decolonisation, and it is noteworthy that his own pragmatic approach (see Dasgupta and Rossi 2021) evolves at the intersection of intercultural production (literary translation) and critical communication pedagogy (literary and linguistic translation studies). As discussed, provocative pedagogy compels Humanities exponents to address their own Humanities subjectivity, for example via their capacity to conceptualise and implement collaborative and other forms of socially responsive and 'emotionally literate' educational projects (see Schroeder 2020). As we will see in Part Four, Sayantan's approach to Participatory Curriculum Development (in Indian Literature and Translation Studies) is a good example of this. Let us continue by addressing one basic problem: the search for value-congruency as well as patterns of interrelation between 'the Humanities' and humanity.

This problem is suggestive of the (differently expressed) situations in which Humanities educators render their own humanity or their own 'emotional literacy' either illegible or disposable especially in terms of the content or the frames of reference, methods, and motivations that inform their work. This malaise has generated a sense of crisis and/or responsiveness amongst some (see Nussbaum 1997; Fry and Tlostanova 2021). In response to these concerns, we can start to think and communicate differently: as members of emergent, plural and overtly 'humanities' collectives (with a lower-case 'h', against Humanity-in-the-singular). These collectives need to be related to our disciplines, to the extent that reformist/actionable texts like this one can also be approached as evidence of proper scholarship concerning (a) one's own subjectivity; (b) the multiplex issues that arise as and when the multiple 'voices' of decolonisation, for example, are translated and heard across cultural, linguistic and social borders; and (c) the interrelation of (a) and (b): as considered in view of the many histories and ideas of responsibility that have emerged as the figure of 'the decolonial' comes to assume a liberated and active presence in education, culture, or modernity at large (see Rycroft 2013; Plummer 2021; Drees 2021; Vazquez 2021).

When we work collectively, the emphasis on the collective is not created at the expense of individual concerns, but in addition to them. The role of the individual in assessing, evolving or critiquing the whole schema of provocation is integral to the many collaborative processes that comprise the community elements of Humanities pedagogy. As such, I anticipate a new era for provocative pedagogy, and I want to inaugurate this as the Provocative Pedagogy Movement (PPM). The phrasing Provocative Pedagogy Movement highlights a number of important features, notably:

1. the mobile nature of the people, ideas, and disciplines involved;

2. the collective, diverse and evolving constituency of the knowledge, understanding and experience being generated; and
3. the prospect of intersubjective (rather than singularly subjective) awareness or consciousness (see Chelstrom 2013).

In my own experience, and in terms of the focus of this text, both the provocations and the pedagogy pertain to the 'Humanities in India Partnerships Programme' that started in 2016 as a core facet of our university-level India Dialogue, and is still in process. Whilst this programme is the main case study, through which many of the ideas and issues have acquired significance, the text is not 'about' this programme per se. Rather it uses this programme to address and then open up some key areas of (self) reflexivity and response, to the extent that one might be able to address PPM as a Pluralist Pedagogy Movement too. As these perspectives have become apparent to me as a co-founder of the 'Humanities in India' collective, I am interested in pursuing PPM as a particular kind of transversal methodology that is ready and willing to engage the interplay between, on the one hand, the values and principles of pluralism and, on the other, the ethical and educational provocations presented in domains such as cultural translation (see Maitland 2017; Katan 2018). In time, the educational qualities of this overtly 'transversal' methodology (see Cole and Bradley 2018) will become clear, as its advocates and exponents move both individually and collectively across and between different registers/scales of power and responsibility, including personal responsibility, academic responsibility, social responsibility, sectoral responsibility and universal responsibility.

Transversality is a critical concept, developed by Felix Guattari and others, which addresses the capacity of different social groups to navigate and change social, cultural, political, educational, gender-based and economic hierarchies, and to do so 'from within'. It has been described as:

> ... an expression of the 'extractions' from the heterogenous levels at which [forms of social capital] operate and the interchanges and inquiries that they enable ... Transversality as such involves continued inquiry into one's own role and those of others in the group ... In contrast to other kinds of collectives which do not question their own existence, the transversal group keeps asking. (Cole and Bradley 2018, 2–3)

In respect of this questioning attitude, the movements between different registers of responsibility themselves become meaningful and therefore teachable. These movements should be empowered by forms of intercultural dialogue and cultural translation. New forms of 'reflexive' responsibility would necessarily evolve as and when different people came to experience the meanings of these intersections in different ways, and these experiences would lend themselves to new kinds of 'inclusive' as well as 'transversal' pedagogy. Teaching and learning informed by PPM would necessarily involve disparate topics, alongside the diverse motivations for addressing these in particular ways, as a means for example to decolonise higher education or to better connect the 'humanities' with global citizenship. Necessarily, one would also need to account for how and why one is drawn into thinking and working with particular 'assemblages' of the social in view of the many subjects, curricula, policies, practices, movements and universities that would be involved in these collective kinds of pluralist experiments (see McKeon 1970; 1978).

As an exponent of PPM, a degree of historical (self) reflexivity is called for. This is because at a basic level provocative pedagogy invites the learner/researcher/subject to respond to a key provocation: what does one make of one's own sense of relatedness (or otherwise) to one's intellectual, social or activist forebears? As provocative, transversal and pluralist pedagogies intend to generate a self-reflexive educational workforce, which is able to process afresh—perhaps via the humanity that is at the heart of 'responsible' eduction and dialogical learning—various histories of social, cultural, and philosophical transformation, this time-bound question is a vital one. Other provocations arise: what can one learn from previous methods and discourses of intellectual, institutional, and political decolonisation, and what is at stake when the sites of resistance, becoming and communication—that necessarily imbricate these discourses within the present—become part and parcel of one's own identity? In this sense, the provocations heralded by diverse histories and historical trajectories upon the present—or, in other words, upon one's own capacity to think, learn, teach or critique in certain ways—beget a series of related provocations. These are developed across an unfolding present by the Humanities practitioner, and concern the comparative and critical work of pedagogy in recognising, disrupting, or enabling these histories. Their salience, in other words, is called into question in the act of making them speak (where possible) to oneself, as someone who is able to listen carefully to their communicative or educational potential, despite being somewhat removed from the earlier or 'original' sites of social action or responsibility (see Rycroft 2016). I will now respond to this history-oriented task, in view of some facets of my own research experience.

Part Three: The voices of the subject and value-congruence

In the process of engendering these communicative possibilities as sites of provocation, a productive ambiguity arises in the terminology of the Humanities 'subject'. Rather than alluding to specific people or specific areas of expertise, the Humanities 'subject' evolves into (and as) a universe of provocation. Workable levels of value-congruency therefore should emerge between and within the subject of knowing (as the learner, educator, or communicator) and the subject of knowledge (as discipline, epistemology, or subject area). As is evident in Ina ter Avest and Cok Bakkar's outline of provocative pedagogy, the concept of value-congruency between individual and social orientations is integral to the 'development' of the educators as 'normative professionals' (Avest and Bakkar 2020, 145). Whilst some Humanities exponents might shudder at the prospect of working or behaving in any kind of normative or prescribed manner, the 'norms' under consideration are co-produced less in accordance with the top-down machinery of either state or institutional governance, and more in view of the social needs and challenges of minority and/or decolonising communities (broadly considered), as well as the diversity of responses that can and should arise in meeting and resolving these challenges.

It is in these productive spaces, therefore, of value-sharing and value-congruence that the educator becomes aware of her or his own capacity to think, as well as to act, in the interests of these communities. This lends itself to difficult yet productive questions, for example about how different people and groups come to perceive and generate actions pertaining to 'agreements' across and between these different interests, and then come to value these in accordance with a whole range of interpretive systems, which may have their own political, historical, or philosophical complexity and subtlety. In terms of 'Indian' anthropology, for example, the interrelation between the anthropological 'subject' (or participant observer) and the social ethos of minorities can be quite pronounced, and subsequently written into the social text (see Rycroft 2017). Given the range of values that are 'out there', whether in terms of group responsibility, or social empowerment, or community heritage, the potential for values to be earmarked, and then discussed or shared as such, is suggestive of a universe of value-creation that demands its own kind of cognition. For example, in becoming cognisant of others' experiences and responses to value pluralism, teachers and learners may become better placed to understand how and why the question of value congruence or, conversely, incongruence (conflicting values) matters in different ways to different people and different institutions (see Vveinhardt 2017). In my own experience, as an anthropological historian—that is to say, as someone whose views on and commitments to history, historiography, and heritage are informed by anthropology, specifically 'Indian' anthropology, as well as those people (past, present, and future) who have a clear stake in the diverse moral, political and representational economies afforded by anthropology—I have been drawn to the concept of value-congruency ever since I first encountered it. As I am hoping to demonstrate, I find this concept both agreeable and productive, in view of its capacity to interrelate the means and the ends of key themes, notably cultural translation, dialogue and responsibility.

My first encounter with the actual concept of value-congruence (as distinct from that which it might allude to or point to) was in Delhi in 2003. I was working as a post-doctoral research fellow, and I was affiliated to the Bharatiya Adivasi Sangamam, or the Indian Confederation of Indigenous and Tribal Peoples (ICITP). I was speaking with one of their Santal (Adivasi) leaders, a grass-roots educator and activist, about plans for our upcoming project that we were in the process of formulating together. As we will see, the question of value-congruence would have an important bearing: not only on our immediate project work, but also on our ongoing capacity to engage value pluralism as the modus operandi for effective social engagement, for example in the emergent domain of Adivasi (or Indigenous) Studies (see Parts Five to Eight). The project concerned the need to document, archive, and analyse the historical and contemporary 'presence' of Santal figures associated with the anti-colonial rebellion or Hul of 1855–56 (see Rycroft 2011; 2014). Having worked in a more archival manner on my PhD, which addressed this historical cataclysm, and its quest for Adivasi Self-rule, from the perspective of both the British East India Company and Subaltern Studies historiography (see Rycroft 2006), I was keen to work once again with contemporary Adivasis, and to do so in a way that might more clearly acknowledge the sacrifices made by their historical insurgents. For the Adivasi activists involved in the ICITP, the concept of value-congruence was integral to the success of their movement as a historic *sangam* (confluence) of past and present socio-political interests (see Rycroft 2011a). It animated the potential for personal-level value-congruence, between themselves as Adivasi activists and the Confederation at large, as well as community-level congruency, between the participating Adivasi organisations and the umbrella-like principles of Adivasi citizenship and Adivasi democracy (see Bijoy 1993; Karlsson 2003; Murmu and Kanhar 2014; Rycroft and Devy 2014; Rycroft 2015; Xaxa 2016; Shrinkhal 2017). At another level, it also broached the more complex spaces of value-congruence between the Confederation and the Republic of India (and its Constitution that recognises the rights of Scheduled Tribes, but does not afford to Adivasis any recognition as Indigenous Peoples), as well as between the Confederation and the United Nations, specifically its Declaration on the Rights of Indigenous Peoples. As such, members of the Confederation have become well-versed in the discourse of value-congruence, and so it should not have come as a surprise to me when one of the Confederation's leaders broached this topic with me, in terms of our joint project.

As someone who had just completed their PhD, on the colonial and imperial responses to the rebellion, and the depiction of these responses in the *Illustrated London News*, I was keen to understand the extent to which the rebellion assumed postcolonial cultural significance in India. I was, of course, familiar with the belated colonial attempt to respond—in the aftermath of the rebellion and its suppression—to the provocation that Santal Customary Law should be formally recognised: as a political and administrative phenomenon requiring distinctive and protective measures (see Rao 2005). I was also familiar with the effects of this process of recognition: in that it (i) resulted in the renaming of the affected districts as the Santal Parganas, (ii) later informed the subsequent Santal Parganas Tenancy Act (and hence this has been seen by some Santals as a partial victory), and (iii) had become submerged in a plethora of colonialist ethnologies that sought to obscure the salience of Santal heritage/historical consciousness to modern India (see, for example, Bradley-Birt 1905). Beyond this, I was starting to become more aware of the politics of 'Indian' anthropology, which aimed from the 1920s onwards to develop a middle way—of dialogue, development and citizenship—between marginalised tribal populations and the emerging nation-state (see Rycroft 2012; 2015a; 2017a). Given the complexity and range of these issues, I thought that my initial concept—to document the statues that commemorated the rebellion in terms of their spatial significance, that is to say as markers of India's subsequent pro-tribal policy of scheduling certain districts (as Scheduled Areas)—was of mutual interest and also practicable. Indeed, it must have been so to have been accepted by the ICITP in terms of their own commitment of resource persons to our project partnership. *But how was this project 'value-congruent' with the Confederation and, by extension, how could a joint project broach different fields of value-congruence?* These were tough, but important, questions to answer. An important dialogue ensued, which I shall paraphrase.

We discussed the proposed project's initial purpose: to document the diverse sites of memory that commemorated the Hul. *Yes, that was fine, but how would the project's findings be made accessible and relevant to the people who commemorate the Hul? Could we contribute to an understanding of the range of historical and memorial processes that involve the Hul, the region's Santal communities, and even India's colonial legacies?* In response to these questions, I delineated some educational prospects, and I aligned these to John Beverley's 'theses' on subalternity (see Beverley 1998). We could also align them to Dipesh Chakrabarty's ideas (2004, first published in 1997) concerning 'minority' histories, especially those aspects of communitarian pasts that are difficult to apprehend through the lens of modern historiography (see Das and Samaddar 2009, 12). As such, the project called into question the work of different representational and communicative modes, as well as the (non) translatability of Santal belief systems. These referred, on the one hand, to the initial cultures of protest and antagonism (that focused on the power of the Santal deity Thakur-jiu to inaugurate and legitimate the rebellion), and, on the other, to subsequent interpretive processes (that were prompted not only by the Hul but also by its suppression, and the re-colonisation of the Santal Parganas). *Yes, that all sounds good. But how could the project actually engage—over the long term—those who commemorate the Hul, and whose lives therefore are impacted by the memory of the revolutionary leaders, such as Sido Murmu?* This was a difficult question, but one that went to the heart of the matter (of value congruence).

Thankfully, the members of the Confederation who were present addressed the issue with me: we should find ways to involve these Adivasi community members in the process of documenting the histories and sites under consideration, in such a way that their involvement would directly inform the future educational communicability of the Hul, in all of its historical, cosmological and ecological complexity. At this point, the project's educational 'heritage' remit was re-made, and the process of co-producing 'Hul Sengel: The Spirit of the Santal Revolution', a mid-length documentary film in Santali, began (Rycroft 2005). This discussion about value-congruence has remained with me ever since, for it focused on the need for my work, as a non-Santal (non-Adivasi) researcher, to complement the broad interests not only of the team of Santal

(Adivasi) social activists that I was directly working with, but also the diverse communities of Santals living in the areas affected by the rebellion and its suppression (see Rycroft 2012a). Although I had of course given some thought to ethical dimensions of the project, I had not addressed these in terms of value-congruence, per se. I was reminded that Chakrabarty's concept of 'subaltern' pasts was premised on the supposed non-translatability of some Santal beliefs; and this following extract demands a closer reading as a means to call into question the historiographic outlook of early exponents of Subaltern Studies:

> In spite of Ranajit Guha's desire to listen to the rebel voice seriously, his analysis cannot offer Thakur the same place of agency in the story of the rebellion that the Santals' statements had given him [via the colonial archive] ... The Santal leaders' own understanding of the rebellion does not directly serve the historical cause of democracy or citizenship or socialism [because these are not reasoned by recourse to the supernatural]. It needs to be reinterpreted ... Here is a case of what I have called subaltern pasts: pasts that cannot ever enter academic history as belonging to the historian's own position (Chakrabarty 2004, 234–35).

As will be shown, this type of historiography is exclusionary. It alludes to value-incongruence and incommensurability in two key areas: (i) between those who believe that the deity Thakur-jiu was responsible for the commencement of the insurgency, and those who do not, and (ii) between those interested in promoting materialist (class-based) accounts of identity and history and those interested in elaborating the more intangible (communitarian) aspects of Adivasi cultural practice. In terms of our project, the issue therefore arose of how to broach these spaces of non-commensurability and related cultures of 'non-translation'. The issue was to some extent linguistic, in that the nuances of the Santali language would need to become prominent in the process of communicating these beliefs and the historical consciousness associated with them. But to my mind the issue transcended language and linguistics to provoke, alongside the question of minority history, a host of social asymmetries. As a team, therefore, we started to chalk out some responses to the issue of non-translatability as well as the deeper problem of value-incongruence.

If Chakrabarty himself had been a believer in the presence of Thakur-jiu, he would not have seen the critical relationship, that emerged between the leaders of the rebellion and this deity, in terms of a 'subaltern' or non-translatable past. The presence of the deity would not have demarcated a domain of incongruent values, between Santal culture and modern knowledge, or between Adivasi consciousness and citizenship. Rather, it would have been addressed as a mode of indigenous historical understanding, in and of itself. Interestingly, I can only share these responses having first broached the issue of value-congruence and incongruence, precisely in these terms and with members of ICITP. In other words, it was in a very direct and productive relationship with value-congruence that the programme of joint research and film-making ensued. It is suggestive of a field of historiography (that is to say Subaltern Studies), that despite the best of intentions may also now require some form of decolonisation, so to speak: to the extent that the belief systems involving Thakur-jiu and other Santal deities might not be excluded from the processes of understanding or writing Adivasi history. Before the issue of congruent values was raised, none of us had properly deliberated upon the different dimensions of 'subaltern' history and memory that featured both in the Jharkhand memoryscape and in Chakrabarty's argument. Initially they did not lend themselves to an aligned response, as the ICITP activists were not very interested in expanding upon any of the issues or provocations (concerning identity, communication, and knowledge) that were raised by Chakrabarty or by earlier exponents of Subaltern Studies. Perhaps there was a sense of fatigue, or even guardedness, concerning the unrelenting levels of interest amongst historians and anthropologists in the insurgent consciousness of 'the Santals' (see Banerjee 2006; Rycroft 2006a). Certainly, the long and difficult representational history of Santal people and culture within mainstream Indian cultures concerned these activists, for it seemed to prove, at least to them, that the process of national decolonisation remained largely incomplete.

In view of this indifference—to the questions and topics raised by the Subaltern Studies collective—I wondered what exactly I could offer. It was only during and after the filming and the transcription that these value-additions could be discerned. What our project offered, at least to the Santali activists involved, was a platform to articulate and harmonise a diverse set of emic or 'insider' perspectives, which emerged from the lived experience of different Santal communities: including descendants of Sido Murmu in Bhognadih village; devotees of 'Sido Murmu' (as a commemorative presence) in surrounding villages; Santali poets, musicians, and dramatists who re-animate the social memory of the Hul; Santal higher education students, with a more remote and indirect access to these histories; and Adivasi activists in other contexts. It was each of these communities' capacity to create—for our imagined audience, and for ourselves—an answer to the question of value-congruence that ensured their inclusion in the film (see Part Five). For the moment, we will shift our focus away from one specific value (namely congruence, or value-congruence) to address some of the many shifts in my own Humanities practice that have occurred since I joined UEA as a Lecturer (now Associate Professor) in the Arts and Cultures of Asia in 2006. Rather than focusing on my own career for the sake of it, I am using it as a prism to address how one's initial experiences, for example in dialogical and participatory pedagogy, lend themselves to an ongoing re-evaluation and re-formulation.

I became invested in broader and different processes of collectivisation, to facilitate the formation in 2015 of my university's India Dialogue, which now involves our 'Humanities in India Partnerships Programme' (see Rycroft 2021) and the Association for University Social Responsibility (see Rycroft et al 2020). As such, the situation of the anthropological 'subject' changed, to meet more directly the needs and interests of like-minded UEA colleagues, students and associates, rather than the soon-to-dissolve ICITP or the descendants and devotees of Sido Murmu, to whom we will return later. Interestingly, the narrative and value of congruency would remain present throughout, even if the process was less markedly anthropological. As an early career fellow, I worked for about seven years in the fields of 'Indian' anthropology and Adivasi Studies, as well as Art History. Around 2014, my professional identity changed, as I responded to some far-sighted collegial advice: to move from this area of specialism towards more interdisciplinary and overtly internationalist milieus. In making these moves, my work within UEA became more conspicuously oriented towards social and humanist, rather than singularly indigenous concerns, and dependent upon a different kind of collaborative energy and vision. What follows is an assessment of this shift: towards the 'Humanities in India' and the transversal methodology that has been employed since.

Part Four: The voices of experience and transversality

Given my own attempts to foster and enhance value-congruence between (a) my teaching and research in the Humanities, (b) my partnership development work, as founder of UEA's India Dialogue, and (c) the specific provocations, communities, and values that have become prominent in one specific part of the India Dialogue initiative—namely the 'Humanities in India' programme—I have also found the idea of methodological pluralism to be helpful. It has enabled me to integrate different facets of my Humanities 'professionalism' at UEA, including teaching such fields as World Art Studies, Indigenous Studies, and Heritage Studies; the significance of my own 'hierarchy' of values, including congruence, to cognate areas such as cultural translation and applied research; as well as a variety of internationalist agendas, encompassing knowledge diplomacy and University Social Responsibility (USR). This work has since evolved into an Association for University Social Responsibility, involving the University of Hyderabad and the UK India Business Council as co-founders alongside the India Dialogue (UEA). We have sought to develop our own focus, in view of the processes of coupling the Humanities in India with international responsibilities of universities (see How Ka Ma and Tandon 2014). This has meant that contributors have been active in coordinating and aligning disciplinary, institutional and multilateral levels of social responsibility, for example in view of their role in addressing the UN's Agenda 2030. As noted by Katie Boone:

> The groundwork for further developing and utilising academic diplomacy to advance the SDGs is already underway. … This will become an enriching and productive endeavour, as it stimulates creative dialogue to enhance common goals, as well as producing productive partnerships and networks. In this way, academic diplomacy is not only a means to an end, but also it is a platform that can continue to be utilised for future goals and topics of concern. (Boone 2020, 37)

In respect of the ground-level role of academia, to facilitate international dialogue and citizen diplomacy, I have found Ina ter Avest and Cok Bakkar's concept of the 'multi-voiced' self to be relevant and empowering, as they have argued that: 'In their identity development, during the development of their multi-voiced self, different "voices" are alternately dominant according to their own perception and valuation, or are given a dominant "voice" by others.' (Avest and Bakkar 2020, 150) This concept gives room for different facets of one's own academic life, interests, and methods to coexist and thereby to become co-productive, in a non-hierarchical and dialogical manner. If they are to be brought into a collaborative Pluralist Pedagogy Movement, these voices and/as provocations must first be experienced at the level of the individual. And they must be discerned as such, which is why this text emphasises the different 'voices' that might inform or enhance our 'multi-voiced' professionalism.

In the process of re-animating these voices and/as provocations, at the cusps of selfhood, education, and society, one can attend to complex textures of social responsibility that arise when the call of the Humanities is heard in various domains of affirmation and assertion. As I have already spent some time focusing on the Santal film project, there is no doubt that some of these additional facets require further clarification.

Let us then move from a study of value-congruence to an exploration of how the terminology of provocative pedagogy has become productive for me. We will reconnect with the Santal film project in the next section. I arrived personally at the term 'provocative pedagogy' in the lead-up to a public talk that I was invited to deliver at Jadavpur University in Kolkata, in January 2020. The full title of the talk was 'The Humanities in India as provocative pedagogy'. As I was then a visiting teaching fellow at Jadavpur, in the Centre for the Translation of Indian Literatures (CENTIL), I was encouraged to work on a number of inter-related educational tasks, which included this talk (as a main event) as well as a number of other teaching events, tutorials, partnership meetings, sustainability tours, and research discussions. Many colleagues at Jadavpur have generated meaningful activities in these areas, whether as a means to develop the JU-UEA partnership or as a means to evolve pre-existing priorities. Integral to the process is Sayantan Dasgupta, as Director of CENTIL whose participation has taken the form of a number of guest talks, joint translation projects, joint research endeavours, and joint workshops (see Humanities in India Partnership Programme 2017; 2018; 2019; Dasgupta and Rycroft 2019; Department of Comparative Literature 2019; Dasgupta and Rossi 2020). In the lead-up to the teaching fellowship, I prepared a presentation on the internationalist concept of 'positive peace' and the historic role of cultural translation in addressing the challenges faced by social minorities in eastern India (see Asiatic Society 2019). During the fellowship, I explored different facets of this institutional response, including the work of 'Indian' anthropology in developing and implementing various state-level Tribal Policies. We could thereby better understand the linkage between Tribal Studies, as a field of education focusing on the social integration of tribal populations, and the broader tenets of social inclusion proffered by various political and academic institutions in the region. These were the focus of my public talk.

I discussed some of the ideological differences between the terminology of Tribe and Adivasi, and the resultant differences of understanding that arise in view of Tribal Studies and Adivasi (Indigenous) Studies. I had previously outlined these differences in my co-edited volume, on the politics of 'becoming' Adivasi (Rycroft and Dasgupta 2011). The main provocation of the talk concerned the issue of how to enhance 'our' responsiveness, as non-Adivasi teachers and learners, to the various kinds of social inclusion that have been proffered by other 'non-Adivasi' people and organisations—such as the nation-state, the university, the United Nations—for the benefit of India's so-called 'tribals'. This was also the theme at my subsequent keynote talk on 'The Question of Human Dignity in Adivasi Studies' (International Seminar on Gandhi and the Adivasi Question), hosted by the Indian Institute of Technology, Gandhinagar, on 1 October, 2020 (see Parts Seven and Eight). In other words, I was trying to summon a social consciousness that was clearly on the margins: as non-Adivasi. There have been important attempts by some Adivasi activists to reverse the binary of 'national' mainstream vis-a-vis 'tribal' margins: into the Adivasi mainstream with non-Adivasi margins (Miri 2014, 59–63). This is part of a longer-term Adivasi agenda to decolonise those relations of power and responsibility that inform the workings of India's federalist structures across India, and that routinely subjugate Adivasi citizens as non-citizens or, perhaps more distressingly, sometimes as non-indigenous or even as non-human (see Rao 2019). So, it was deemed worthwhile to broach some of the contours and limitations of being 'non-Adivasi'. What are the roles and responsibilities of predominantly non-Adivasi organisations and interest groups in defining and implementing policies of social inclusion, such as affirmative action? If, in respect of my talk, pedagogic provocation was 'the means', then the cultivation of a deeper engagement with value pluralism and value-congruence could be seen to be 'the ends'. In realising these objectives, a number of issues surrounding cultural translation were also raised, as will now be explored.

I approached my work with the Department of Comparative Literature through the prism of cultural translation.[1] This focus evolved in view of some preliminary conversations on this topic—and its significance to linguistic and literary translation,

[1] The teaching fellowship was made possible by the Department of Comparative Literature at Jadavpur University, and its recognition within the Ministry of Human Resource Development's centrally sponsored scheme known as RUSA (Rashtriya Ucchatar Shiksha Abhiyan, or National Higher Education Mission). The cultivation of different approaches to translation has been integral to the work of the Department for decades. The Centre for Translation of Indian Literatures (CENTIL) exists as a centre within Comparative Literature at Jadvapur University, and under the leadership of Sayantan and others, including Aveek Majumdar, it has focused on the translation of indigenous literary and cultural texts. As with CENTIL, the Department makes good use of the 'translation workshop' approach, and over the years it has involved languages like Tamil, Malayalam, Punjabi, Marathi, Asamiya and Odia. Working in conjunction with the Centre of Advanced Study programme, members of the Department (with Professor Ipshita Chanda at the helm) and CENTIL have also engaged closely with Nepali, and Nepali literature, as facets of India's (in addition to Nepal's) linguistic heritage.

and other fields—with Sayantan Dasgupta. Our conversations encompassed various possibilities and questions, such as 'How and to what extent do the Five Principles that underpin the UN's Agenda 2030 translate into the seventeen Sustainable Development Goals?', and 'What are the prospective roles of intercultural mediation and translation in apprehending these Five Principles in different communities?' Working on the premise that different kinds of (methodological, philosophical, or value) pluralism accrue both social and academic efficacy through processes of mediation and/or translation, Sayantan and others have become invested in addressing the 'Humanities in India' agenda in this light. In the lead-up to my Jadavpur visit, Sayantan held the post of visiting fellow at the University of East Anglia. There we sought to connect UEA's commitment to the Global Challenges not only to his work on minority literatures but also to our burgeoning 'Humanities in India' ethos. In our specific case, as formal representatives of the JU-UEA partnership, the shared challenge under consideration corresponded to the need to question whether and how the processes of diversifying, decolonising, or regenerating the Humanities equated in any sense to the multiple discourses of peace, justice, human dignity, global citizenship, indigeneity and sustainability that are addressed by the United Nations (also see Part Seven). Beyond the UN, they are also addressed by academics and subject-areas linked to these discourses, whether in respect of 'global challenges' or the seventeen Sustainable Development Goals (see UNESCO Editorial 2017; Sustainable Development Solutions Network 2017; Rycroft et al 2020). As previously intimated, it is in these spaces of global and local responsibility, as well as of academic and social praxis, that the concept of transversality may become productive. I had much earlier been involved in a UN-facing consultation on Adivasis in India, and the question of how and why India is able to involve, via political and cultural decentralisation, different 'scales' of indigenous and national governance (Bellier 2010). So, in view of my earlier work with ICITP, which led to another phase of partnership work in 2005, namely the Santal Hul 150 Forum—that aimed to bring together a host of Adivasi/non-Adivasi activists and Adivasi/non-Adivasi scholars from different parts of eastern India for a dialogue on resistance and 'inclusive' history—I was able to conjoin multiple entry points within this fellowship programme.

These dialogues are still ongoing, but they all now assume new levels of coherence and compatibility. As exponents of the 'Humanities in India' team, we have broadened the equation to involve not only the UN discourses but also less governance-heavy (that is, more people-centric and/or grass-roots) arenas of social action and social responsibility. In some ways, these are not necessarily in opposition, as the worldwide community of Indigenous Peoples has been heralded as a major stakeholder group by those responsible for the implementation of the UN's Agenda 2030 for the Implementation of the Sustainable Development Goals. Interestingly, the 'Humanities in India' team ethos, alongside the expertise of those involved in its implementation, has yielded another set of interests, concerning the congruency or otherwise between (a) 'our' kinds of approaches to social sustainability, and (b) the institutional commitment of our universities to the implementation of the SDGs. Whether as partnership point persons, or as members of this Humanities collective, we have deemed it necessary to retain a commitment to matters of value-congruence and intercultural translation, in terms of:

1. our simultaneously discipline-specific and institutional contexts;
2. the practical and theoretical dimensions of these simultaneously experienced contexts; and
3. the pedagogic salience of all of these interconnected concerns.

In sum, we are moving slowly but purposefully towards a Humanities-wide engagement with different levels of global and social responsibility. Whilst Sayantan has been advocating for the translation of India's minority and oral literatures (see Dasgupta 2018; 2021; Ishani Dutta 2019), my own response has been to develop a methodology that reflects the dynamic workings of these comparative value systems and various transversal journeys. Hence I settled upon the terminology of provocative pedagogy, and spoke about this at Jadavpur University in early January, 2020. As I would discover, and as I have already outlined, I have not been alone in exploring this idea.

This current text is being written more than two years after that event. It therefore renders the concept of provocative pedagogy slightly differently, as it is able to absorb some important developments that have occurred during this interim period, notably our putting together of a series of Dialogues on Decolonisation (Rycroft 2021), as well as the aforementioned publication by Ina ter Avest and Cok Bakkar. Inasmuch, I have renamed the text 'Humanities in India as Pluralist Pedagogy'. This is not so much a movement away from provocative pedagogy. Rather it is a deliberate attempt to align that which may evolve through a Provocative Pedagogy Movement with broader concerns, notably value pluralism, cultural pluralism, and methodological pluralism. Since the talk in January 2020, much of the world has been negatively impacted by the Covid pandemic. Rather than continuing with the teaching exchanges, members of the Humanities in India group developed some virtual initiatives. Of these, two have become significant to me. First, there has been the initiation, within the rubric of UEA's commitment to University Social Responsibility, of an academic response group to the work and intellectual legacies of Richard McKeon. Secondly, there has been the interactive series of Dialogues on Decolonisation. In early 2021, the 'Humanities in India' steering group that comprised Sayantan, myself, Jon Cook (Emeritus Professor, Modern Literature), Rukmini Bhaya Nair (Professor of Poetry, IIT, Delhi) and Samir Kumar Das (Professor of Polical Science, University of Calcutta) decided to join hands to implement this series. In a sense, it is our own collective provocation, that summons the following concerns:

1. that dialogue, in different forms, can become the source not only of understanding but also of partnership,
2. that decolonising higher education is an uneven, complex and difficult to solve possibility, especially when it requires wholesale sectoral as well as subject-level reforms, and
3. that provocations can and should be articulated collectively, requiring of the collective not only a careful but also a distributed and de-centred responsiveness to social challenges and related forms of academic responsibility.

Interestingly, in different and diverse ways, the concept of provocative pedagogy seems to resonate in each of these domains of Humanities praxis. In due course, we may even be in a position to implement it across different universities as a 'new' curriculum option. As a collective, we also take very seriously other outputs and other approaches to Humanities pedagogy, such as Rukmini's advocacy of the LEAF movement in India (Liberal Education in the Arts Fields) and Samir's development of 'peace' as a social value in/for the Humanities (see Nair 2019; Das 2021). Since our first wave of curriculum development meetings in 2015–17, we articulated the 'Humanities in India' as our common agenda and have retained this focus ever since. We have involved a new colleague in the steering group, namely Prof Indranil Acharya of Vidyasagar University, who has been key to the formation in eastern India of the People's University movement, via his work with the People's Linguistic Survey of India. In the domain of India's minority languages, this has important parallels with the earlier Santal Hul 150 Forum: notably in its capacity to make Adivasi activists central to the reevaluation of linguistic and cultural exclusion, inclusion, documentation, interpretation, and pedagogy (see Acharya 2017; Gupta and Padel 2018). The key point here, in respect of the theme of the Jadavpur talk, is that clear opportunities are arising to properly inhabit meaningful 'non-Adivasi' spaces (also see Parts Six and Eight). These are not 'non-Adivasi' spaces in the sense that they do not involve Adivasis. I would say that the reverse is true. The focus on the 'non-Adivasi' is a self-conscious response to the fact that there are now important pedagogic movements being led by Adivasi activists and representatives, meaning that non-Adivasi learners should be encouraged to rethink their relationship to these movements. In using the term 'non-Adivasi' in this way, I would like to anticipate a new era of collective self-awareness concerning the evolving relationship between mainstream higher education and Adivasi constituencies in India.

In broader terms, when we speak of the 'Humanities in India', we are in fact attempting to highlight the present and future significance of:

1. Humanities disciplines, and associated fields of experience, collectivisation, communication and education to different social groupings;
2. India-based Humanities exponents, and their specific expertise, insights, knowledge, and creativity to Humanities departments outside South Asia;
3. the convergences of different types and remits of social responsibility, as an educational provocation concerning the broader currents of social change and social consciousness, to faculty and students alike;
4. the particular socio-cultural phenomena, such as cultural translation, anti-colonial resistance, internationalism, and global citizenship education as departure points for 'provocative pedagogy'; and
5. the broader call, or voice and resonance, of cultural, methodological and value pluralism to diverse stakeholders, including those beyond the Humanities, who may be able to transform 'humanism' to make it more value-congruent with the many constituent parts of humanity, especially those parts that are routinely ignored or marginalised by Higher Education Institutions.

In early 2022 the 'Humanities in India' steering group released an e-booklet that covers the 2021 series of Dialogues on Decolonisation (Rycroft 2021). This has become the focus for a new phase of joint teaching, with Vidyasagar University, as well as the focus for a Bangla (Bengali language) intervention, involving the University of Calcutta, on the prospect of translating these dialogues. This intervention raises the issue of why some academic resources concerning social justice and decolonisation in India are only available in Bengali or conversely in English. It addresses the specific relation between important linguistic terms, such as justice or decolonisation, and their historical and academic currency, whether in Bengali or English. In sum, we are concerned with facilitating a critical consciousness around how and why the Humanities are humanised and decolonised in different ways, in different places. In view of my capacity now to engage the Santal film project within the parameters of this broader Humanities ethos, let us return to it to assess how and why 'the spirit of the Santal revolution' responds to other pedagogic concerns, such as cultural translation.

Part Five: The voices of memory and commemoration

As noted in Part Three, the film 'Hul Sengel: The Spirit of the Santal Revolution' documents how the rebellion features in the historical consciousness and cultural landscape of northern Jharkhand. As a collaborative endeavour, it also provides evidence of an emergent congruence of value: between those involved in the film and the sites at which the revolution evolved, as well as between histories of survival and cultures of commemoration. From the wreckage of insurgency and counter-insurgency, a post-conflict social history emerged that—from the point of view of those closely affiliated to the Hul—attests to the ongoing social and political presence of the revolutionaries. As is explored in the film, the sites of the rebellion have evolved into new spaces of belonging, to the extent that the Santal Parganas (the districts involved in the rebellion) feature alongside the descendants of the revolutionaries less as spatial contexts and more as historical witnesses. During the phase before the rebellion, it was the Santal labourers who literally made the landscape around the Damin-i-Koh (the so-called skirt of the Rajmahal hills). During the rebellion and its suppression, this contested landscape enabled the insurgent movement to develop in the ways that it did: that is to say between districts (the various Parganas), between the hills and the plains, and between Santal and non-Santal insurgents (see Rycroft 2006). And in the wake of the Hul, it was the landscape that absorbed the blood of the fallen and provided the gruesome architecture for colonial punishments (for example the use of trees to hang the insurgent leaders). And in more recent times, it was this same contested landscape that would feature in both colonial and national attempts to integrate Adivasi land rights, first via the policy of Excluded and Partially Excluded Areas, and then within the Fifth Schedule in India's Constitution (see Rycroft 2012b; 2017).

The challenge of representing this complexity was beyond us, as film-makers. We did, however, respond carefully to the metaphorical and narrative potential of the landscape. The liminal space of the veranda, notably the veranda of the family home of the descendants of Sido Murmu, is featured in the film. It is a space that is not only private (in that it belongs to the family), but also social and public (in terms of its capacity to welcome both Adivasi and non-Adivasi guests, and to become the site, just as it was in the lead up to the rebellion, of provocation and communication). Just as the leaders and first wave of insurgents congregated at this family home, to honour their deities and to envisage a decolonial future, so it now houses their commemorative statues, which family members rescued and re-housed, after they were decommissioned from a nearby public memorial. These, and a wide array of other public commemorative statues, provide for different Santal groupings in the region an important bridge not only between past and present, but also between myth and reality, and between the human and non-human realms. In respect of these important concerns, the film also situates a number of beliefs and spiritual practices that are connected to these sites and realms, such as the field at Bhognadih, which is where the rebellion started at the behest of (Thakur-jiu and) the revolutionary brothers on 30th June 1855.

These beliefs pertain to the elevated position that Sido Murmu and Kanhu Murmu, alongside other figures involved in the rebellion, hold in contemporary Adivasi society: as literal and environmental embodiments of justice, resilience, and truth. It is not that these values are specific to these figures, or even to these communities, rather that there is a powerful and meaningful convergence between them. It is a convergence that attests to the ideal of Adivasi political authority, as expressed through the Manjhi-Pargana systems of decentralised democracy. Just as Chakrabarty became concerned at the difficulty of writing the deity Thakur-jiu (as a creation deity) into a materialist history, so the representational dilemmas engulfing social and historical agency can extend, in the eras after the Hul and its suppression, also to Sido Murmu and Kanhu Murmu as the focal points of contemporary commemoration and devotion (see Rycroft 2011). This is because they are now apprehended by Adivasi devotees as immortal. As they did not die during the suppression of the rebellion, their immortality invokes an important timeline of continuity, which has serious repercussions concerning the multiple (social, political, cultural, environmental and spiritual) dimensions of Adivasi Self-rule, and the potential for these dimensions either to be recognised and taken seriously or, alternatively, to be rendered marginal and meaningless. In terms of a Humanities corollary, the issue is less about questioning the supposedly untranslatable nature of Thakur-jiu (in terms of Santal history), and more about understanding the human character, and political and pedagogic potentiality, of this overtly 'Adivasi' social memory. If one is involved in rendering these beliefs and memories meaningful, one is invested in an overtly intersubjective process, which requires fuller explanation.

As immortal entities, Sido Murmu and Kanhu Murmu assume a comparable presence (to contemporary Santals) as

Thakur-jiu did in the eyes, hearts and minds of these leaders in 1855. So, in focusing on the creative 'presence' of Sido Murmu and Kanhu Murmu as revolutionaries and as contemporary yet unseen leaders, one is able to apprehend how and why the value-congruence that existed between the insurgents and their deity may be transmittable and meaningful (via its cultural translation, and intermediation by devotees) to Santal/ Adivasi communities today, as explored in the film by Rup Chand Murmu (see Rycroft 2012a). One is therefore obliged to disrupt Chakrabarty's influential contention that Thakur-jiu is untranslatable. This is because the ICITP grouping has been able to develop, via the film-making process, a context for the Santali transmission of a two-way translation: first of Thakur-jiu into Sido Murmu, via the evidence that is shared in the film concerning the latter's immortality, and then the re-translation of 'Sido Murmu' (as an iconic rather than a historical figure) into the social memory of the Santal Parganas via a spirit of commemoration, which is regularly activated, for example during the Hul Maha (Day of Revolution) events that are held on June 30th. So, we are involved in a process of active interpretation that is less concerned with whether or not Thakur-jiu is translatable, and is more concerned with how we can apprehend and understand the complex political, intangible, and environmental power of 'Sido Murmu' and others. One might even contend that the film 'Hul Sengel' defines, legitimates and activates this discourse of Adivasi social responsibility.

Importantly, the film served the purpose of sharing, primarily for Santali-speakers on the occasion of the 150th anniversary of the Hul, a narrative of discontent that made present concerns and historical injustices mutually intelligible.

It has been widely seen in the region, and it has affirmed the (indigenous) educational authority of many of the speakers whose views and testimonies were featured. These focused on the spaces of co-existence between history and present, between Thakur-jiu and the leaders, between sites of trauma and narratives of becoming. The insights that evolved through the process of making the film were, of course, not available to Chakrabarty when he wrote his own thesis on the untranslatability of the 'subaltern' facets of Santal pasts. But the point is this: that neither Thakur-jiu (in 1855) nor 'Sido Murmu' (as an immortalised figure in the present) are considered subaltern by those who recognise, understand or value them. Rather, they are highly present, highly vocal, and highly resonant. One may be thankful to Chakrabarty for raising the initial point: that as an immaterial presence it is near impossible to write Thakur-jiu into a 'minority' history. As we found out during our project, if one switches one's orientation towards social memory, as the necessary prerequisite for the constitution of that 'minority', one can move beyond this contention, to claim otherwise: that it is difficult, but not impossible to involve both Thakur-jiu and Sido Murmu in an Adivasi 'present' that aligns multiple temporalities. These temporalities involve historical, commemorative, political, mythical and narrative coordinates. As such, they enable spaces of affinity and value-congruence to develop, for example between Thakur-jiu, Sido Murmu, his descendants, devotees, and anyone willing and able to listen to their views and shared experiences. This is not so much an anthropological representation as an Adivasi reality, involving Adivasis and non-Adivasis alike. To my mind, it is a reality that also takes us back to one of our starting points: the search for 'patterns of value and responsibility'. But it transports us in a way that also complicates the sense of order or stability that is presumed by the notion of cultural patterning (which itself was a common anthropological metaphor, during McKeon's era). This is partly because it alludes to a sense of value and responsibility that is neither fully disclosed nor fully translated; and it is also because its partial disclosure and partial reinterpretation are co-dependent on a culture of responsiveness and mutual respect, which is not guaranteed.

In view of my role in co-producing this film and disseminating this non-patterned reality, another level of value-congruency emerged at the moment of screening the film at Bhognadih Village on June 30th 2005, that is to say during the massive Hul Maha commemoration that took place in the fields that witnessed the start of the rebellion on June 30th 1855. Just as the film opened with the scene of Bitiya Hembram, a fifth generation descendent of Sido Murmu, walking with her grandson—also named Sido—to the commemorative plinth at Bhognadih, so Bitiya and I walked side by side to conduct our own ceremony in the hours leading up to the outdoor film-screening. We had spent some time chatting beforehand, and she seemed a bit overwhelmed at the size of this particular annual gathering. After our short walk from her house to a nearby commemorative plinth, which housed two sculptures depicting the leaders of the rebellion, she presented me with a handful of soil from the field. She had seen, as I was carrying some garlands, that I was about to honour these leaders and their legacies. Perhaps she wanted to thank me for the gifts (some brass vessels) that I had given her family as a token of my appreciation for their role in co-hosting the Hul Maha. At any rate, the gift of the soil seemed, at the time, to be a wonderfully spontaneous and personal gesture. This was dutifully and gratefully accepted, and it was a significant moment, at least for me. It suggested that value-congruency had started to exist between the descendants based at Bhognadih and the film-makers.

In terms of this discussion about value-congruence, this symbolic exchange has remained with me as a vivid and ever-present memory. The exchange was interpreted at the time, by our Santal activist colleagues, within a broader Adivasi culture of taking-the-oath. This was directly referred to in the film, by Rup Chand Murmu, who is one of Bitiya's family members. He is the one who most eloquently expressed (in the film) both the trauma and the prescience of Sido's immortality. He would later articulate the solidarity that exists amongst the diverse Santal groupings who have taken-the-oath. It is the oath of defining one's political and historical consciousness: as a direct affirmation not only of the Hul, its cosmology, its legacy, and its prescience, but also of Adivasi-hood, as well as everything that this stands for, in terms of future communication, education, knowledge, human dignity and action. Whilst I am prepared to go on record as saying that I am to a large extent on-board with this oath, especially when I am thinking and working in respect of these Adivasi issues (see Chandra 2015), I accepted the soil as a meaningful gift, rather than as part and parcel of an oath-driven commitment! Back then, it conjured forth the idea that the place could, alongside the people, witness diverse kinds of events, and become embedded within the universe of social responsibility that we have been addressing.

In its capacity to speak to Bitiya, so Bitiya wanted to ensure that the Santal Parganas could speak to me. Given this ecological premise, one is reminded of other kinds of pilgrimage experiences, as well as the broader qualitative and reciprocal dimensions of *darsana*, that enable participants to move beyond fixed binary relations, for example of devotee and deity, or worshipper and worshipped, as a means of instituting a more de-centred sense of interrelation, co-presence and coexistence. The voice of the soil, to me, came across as a form of speech that was direct and, in quite literal terms, non-reciprocal. It demanded of me a quite different response from the many 'words' and 'relations' and 'sites' that had previously been conveyed during the course of 'Hul Sengel'. And it demanded a response that was also distinct from all of the previous (pre-2003 to 2005) relationships that I had developed with the soil of Jharkhand, notably those that were premised on the use, amongst Adivasi women, of clay in domestic mural patterning. Bitiya's gift of the soil seemed to underscore her acknowledgement of the productive and holistic work of 'place', as inherent to those processes of Adivasi cultural production and activism, notably the commemoration of 'Sido Murmu' and Thakur-jiu, to which we had become attuned as the 'spirit of the Santal revolution'. Intriguingly, however, it also seemed to disrupt the complexity of all of these kinds of processes. It was its simplicity, as well as its instantaneous nature, that yielded its power. In the filmmaking process we had been concerned with numerous 'staging' nuances, such as how fast the 'witnesses' should walk, how they would sit, how loud they should talk, where the microphones should be, and so on. Even though these were largely organic processes, the gifting was a delightfully light and casual antidote to the organisation that defined many of our previous interactions. On reflection, it makes sense as the interpersonal equivalent of the single word that was spoken by Bitiya, to the filmmakers, after she had viewed the film for the first time. 'How was it?', she was asked. With a self-deprecating smile, and a quick sideways glance came the response: 'Moj'. (It was all 'fine'.)

It may seem slightly odd, in a discussion about value-congruence and dialogue, for me to demarcate this line of distinction, between 'receiving the gift' and 'taking the oath'. To my mind, however, it is important to articulate the terms of my response: to present an accurate personal account. I was not under any obligation to accept the gift but, of course, I wanted to and I needed to, and so I did. I was not in a position to accept the full prescriptions of the oath, because I did not know about them at the time and then, as now, I would not be able to do them the kind of justice that they deserve. I am a believer in the complex ecology of responsibility, in the sacrifice of the insurgents, and in the capacity of the Santal Parganas to continue to speak and to provoke. I am therefore also a believer in the need to shift the attention of the Humanities, not so much away from 'subaltern' history per se, but towards the 'indigenous' humanism of such arenas as Adivasi cultural and political heritage. So, one might say that I am a respectful ally of Sido Murmu (the historic insurgent) rather than his historian, and a friendly associate of 'Sido Murmu' (the diety) rather than his devotee. I know what it means to hold the soil of the Santal Parganas in my hand, and to be in the presence of different Santal deities and *bongako* (immaterial entities). But I am not 'of the soil', as I could not tell you anything of real significance about these entities or the presences they afford (see Mitra and Jha 2015), or even begin to explain the cosmological significance of the oaths and futures in question.

So, the moral of the story is to accept and, where relevant, to respect and work productively with the different levels and meanings of value-congruency that exist in diverse contexts. And the unresolved purpose of the story is to highlight how, as someone who is coming to terms with the prospects of 'reflexive' responsibility, value-congruence can assume a life and a materiality of its own. Our 'humanities' pedagogy may interact with Adivasi histories, experiences, memories, narratives and beliefs, but it cannot equate to them. These phenomena have their own power, presence, and provocative potential. Indeed, an encouragement of 'higher' learning with, for, and by 'Adivasi' pedagogues may be a crucial next step. To some extent, the film is evidence that this kind of pedagogy is possible. For now, it is a question of understanding how these phenomena may persist as features of a more overtly humanised and/or indigenised Humanities education.

Part Six: The voices of complexity and community

In view of these complex issues, one can arrive at a proposition: that pluralist and provocative pedagogy can, does and should encompass multiple forms of, and attitudes towards, 'human' and non-human as well as Adivasi and 'non-Adivasi' education and culture. Taken together, these are some of the constituent elements of 'humanities' subject-hood. To discern and enable specific 'patterns' of either values or responsibility may, at this stage, be too optimistic. Rather, let us broach the complexity of this evolving constitution and aim to arrive at an understanding of what this means for us. In view of the value that we afford to our own responsiveness—to existing Humanities discourses that address relevant social fields, philosophies, or histories—an emphasis on intersubjectivity (alongside subjectivity) can become productive. The concept of intersubjective pedagogy can be linked to questions of 'responsible' consciousness as well as to 'contemplative' research (see Gunnlaugson 2017). This is because it helps learners, as well as those responsible for nurturing pluralist pedagogy, to move beyond 'postmodern' approaches to pluralism.

As Joanne Gozawa has rightly noted, postmodern pluralism is a movement that tends to focus on the 'plural realities that arise from the variation in historical-cultural experiences among different groups' (Gozawa 2017, 64). These variations are no doubt very important. Nowadays, however, we may also generate value in embracing the possibilities and dynamics of 'our mutuality, our reciprocal self-making, our common experiences' (Gozawa 2017, 65). This alludes to the intersubjective 'turn', which is thought to occur 'when knower and that which is to be known are [constituted] as mutual subjects in an abiding objective presence. … Selves and the physical-cosmic-social world in which they are embedded are in view at once.' (Gozawa 2017, 64–65) We are thereby encouraged to understand subjectivity less singularly, whether in terms of the individuals, disciplines, or histories involved, and more in view of their interrelation and capacity to co-produce, for example, an ethic of shared responsibility in/for/with the 'humanities'. To my mind, this 'movement' of provocative pedagogy from the realm of the individual, to the realm of the collective, and back and forth, anticipates and excites new assemblages of the social, the moral, and the political. Considered in these emergent and axiological terms, the universe of transversal responsibility becomes multi-dimensional, multi-cultural, multi-disciplinary, multi-temporal, and multi-sited.

We, the 'Humanities in India' team, have each arrived at a point where we can re-evaluate our common agendas in ways that develop their historical and social salience and congruence. The historical legacies of many Humanities philosophers, and the evolving ethos of social responsibility among educational institutions, organisations, and collectives in India, are never far from our minds (see Bilimoria 2017; Miri 2017). Their willingness to address the practical, conceptual, and comparative dimensions of modern Humanities pedagogy—as well as the attendant discourses of humanism, secularism, cosmopolitanism, human rights, human dignity, humanitarianism, anthropology and cultural diversity (see Hardison 1972)—remains relevant. Like many of our intellectual and ethical forebears, our collective provocations concern the future of the 'humanities': as an enmeshment of congruent experiences, expressions, values, ideals, methods, ideas and languages. Throughout this text, I have been alluding to the value of pluralist methodologies, that is to say methodologies that consciously involve a number of contrasting processes, ideas, or objectives. And as this text is based on the write-up of my public talk at Jadavpur University, it is only right that I should reflect in detail on one of the key issues, namely being at the margins of the Adivasi movement. I deem it appropriate to do so in the company of someone who was an early exponent of provocative pedagogy in India, and who I taught alongside as a visitor at Jadavpur University: Pashupati Prasad Mahato. He became well-known in India's higher education and field-based contexts as someone who had serious reservations about the history of Othering that classified 'Mahatos' (including Kudmi and Kurmi Mahatos) as members of the Other Backward Classes (OBCs), within India's Constitution (see Somanboina and Ramagoud 2022). Even before the Mandal Commission, which advocated the enhancement of affirmative action for OBCs (see Agrawal and Aggarwal 1991), Pashupati was very active in eastern India's educational and cultural politics. Here, he developed a conspicuously embodied and vocal engagement as a 'non-Adivasi' in spaces driven by various forms of affirmative action and indigenous cultural heritage.

Although he saw himself as an Adivasi, he questioned everything as an OBC. Therefore, one might be able to address his socio-cultural work and educational presence in terms of participatory citizenship (see Mohanty and Tandon 2006). This occurred as and when he encountered Adivasi value-systems and histories as a 'non-Adivasi', in that he was attempting to realign the space of the Other (as OBC, or non-Adivasi) within a more authentic and radical self-hood, as Adivasi. Many of Pashupati's educational and anthropological contributions involved this kind of nuanced, complex and disruptive social performance, with a view to making his anthropological identity and his focus of study (identity-formation in modern India), mutually expressive, intelligible and congruent. There are at least two dimensions of Othering, therefore, that require some further consideration: (i) the spaces of otherness that emerge as and when Adivasi (or Scheduled Tribe) and Dalit (or Scheduled Caste) identities become the main focus for identity-construction, to render those communities that are 'backward', but that are non-Adivasi or non-Dalit, as their significant Others; and (ii) the question and construction of the Other as produced, for example, within emic Adivasi perspectives. The 'developmental' idea of backwardness, of course, legitimates the opposite notion—of progress—as well as (a) its institutionalisation, via colonial and/or national value systems, and (b) related forms of 'inclusive' governance. A two-fold process of Othering occurs: first in terms of rendering the indigenous and downtrodden communities 'backward', and secondly in the capacity of the ST and SC groups to delineate certain kinds of social exclusion that create their own spheres of difference and differentiation, as compared with the Other 'backward castes' or 'backward classes'. We will now explore what this meant to Pashupati.

As a cultural anthropologist based at the Anthropological Survey of India, central Kolkata, Dr Mahato was well-known to many of the academic and social communities that I have been referring to. In the mid-1990s, he was my first academic guide in India, and he would later give the keynote speech at the launch of my monograph, *Representing Rebellion* (Rycroft 2006). He helped me to conduct some preliminary research into the arts and cultures of various non-Adivasi communities in West Bengal/Jharkhand, notably Purulia District (Rycroft 1996). I use the term 'non-Adivasi' advisedly, as their economy has historically speaking been derived from their close association with Adivasi villagers, meaning that their cultural identity has developed in respect of their capacity to interact productively with Santal, Bhumij and Munda people. In these precise terms, it may be instructive to rethink some of Pashupati's own work, as this can help us to understand his own subject-position as a member of a lineage community (Mahato) who have come to see themselves as Mulvasi (Original Inhabitants) or Adivasi (Earliest Inhabitants), but whose formal designation is OBC. The political ramifications of being part of the OBC community have been near to the surface of higher education in India since the late 1990s, when the Mandal Commission involved OBC groups in an affirmative action package for enhancing social inclusion (see Robin 2009; Kumar 2014; Mandal 2021).

In writing this text, I have been able to reflect upon various experiences of teaching and learning at Jadavpur University in accordance not only with their broader timespans, but also in respect of the evolving textures of educational 'inclusion'. In 2015, I was historian-in-residence at the Department of History, and vividly remember co-teaching with Pashupati on the subject of subaltern resistance in India. Whilst I spoke about Birsa Munda and his memory in Jharkhand (see Part Eight), Pashupati waxed lyrical about this and other indigenous social movements. It was a very powerful moment for me, as we seemed to have come full-circle since our original interactions in Kolkata and Purulia twenty years earlier. At the same time, I was also honoured to deliver a keynote talk at Dr Mahua Sarkar's international conference on 'Environment and the Adivasi World' (Rycroft 2017a). It would be the last time that I would ever speak to Pashupati (as he passed away before Covid). Whilst these are inevitably sad memories, they are also touched by a real sense of wonder, particularly in view of his unique capacity to inspire audiences and learners through his interweaving of the Jhumur (folk song) traditions of eastern India and contemporary anthropological concerns (see Mahato 1987; Chatterji 2004).

When I was an affiliate of Pashupati in the 1990s, I was asked to proofread some preliminary drafts of an English translation of his work on the historical and cultural connections between Adivasi and agrarian communities in eastern India. We sat for hours in his office in the Anthropological Survey, going through hand-typed pages derived from an early draft of *Jharkhander Hor-Mitan (Kherowal) Samajik Savyata: Silpa Chetna O Joban Rasabhodh* (Socialisation of Kheroals in Jharkhand). We mulled over different ideas and suggestions concerning the use of specific English-language phrases in this draft translation. It was a useful induction for me, into the work of anthropological mediation and communication. Pashupati was my first teacher in 'Indian' anthropology, and he would remain very interested in the capacity of anthropology to engender cultural critique and social responsibility. As a student of Surajit Sinha, he pioneered both cultural anthropology and auto-ethnography, and sought to rewrite the discourse of identity in Jharkhand: this would focus more on the lived realities of specific communities, and less on inherited or administrative typologies (Mahato 2003). This provocation made a lasting impact on me.

For Pashupati, the idea of indigeneity in India should not be premised on the (false) dichotomy of 'tribe' versus 'caste' (see Sinha 1965; Upadhyay and Pandey 1993, 479–80). Rather it should respond to the historical relevance—to the people of the region, and hence to him as an anthropologist—of the role of the Adivasi (Indigenous/tribal) communities in defining, and then developing over time, diverse socio-political, economic and cultural relations with so-called non-Adivasi or neighbouring communities, and vice versa (Mahato 2003). Of course, in respect of this current text, these processes would necessarily develop their own social, philosophical and educational borderlands, in terms of (the movement between) what I have been referring to as the 'non-Adivasi' and the 'Adivasi'. For Pashupati, the formal dividing lines that characterise the divisions between so-called Scheduled Tribes and so-called 'non-tribals' are not only historically and culturally inaccurate, but also they are evidence of the hegemonic processes and power-relations that over time have 'silenced' the values, for example of social equality, that these historic communities had generated (Mahato 2000). In an effort to stimulate or provoke further understanding of his thesis, Pashupati heralded a new term for this more inclusive and equal society: Horo-Mitan. This was featured in the title of the draft translation, which I was asked to assess. Derived from the indigenous Mundari and Santali vocabulary that, as it happens, also informs the spoken dialect of many of the region's non-Adivasis, the terminology of Horo-Mitan (or Hor-Mitan) may be translated as Human-Friend. Given its integral significance to Pashupati's vision, we need to be prepared to develop a closer analysis of this term. For any anthropologist, or any person sensitive to the significance of cultural and linguistic details and nuances, it will always be productive to question the presence of 'the human' in the Humanities: How does it figure? How and why are its configurations created, conveyed and contested in different ways? Why, as 'humanities' educators, are we encouraged to work either with or against inherited or 'legacy' notions of humankind?

In linguistic terms, the term Horo or Hor refers in Austro-Asiatic languages variously to 'People', 'Human', 'Us' (Mahato 1997). In the history of indigenous belonging and becoming, for many Santali and Mundari speakers the term is loaded: not only does it refer to the sense of belonging within the Adivasi community, but also it refers by implication to a sense of differentiation given the historical experience of being Othered, whether by later settlers, by colonisers, by industrialists, or whoever (see Pfeffer and Behera 1997, 112–14). In accordance with his own sense of his own indigeneity, and as a member of a 'Mahato' community that has existed historically in a direct association with the Adivasi-led Horo-Mitan culture, Pashupati also sought to call into question the 'negative' binary that would inform a popular understanding of the term Horo. It is a negative binary because it is normally used, by Mundari and Santali speaking Adivasis, to refer to the Adivasi side of an 'Adivasi versus non-Adivasi' sense of opposition, which is termed Horo-Diku (or Self-Other) that is to say 'us versus them' (see Macdougall 1977; Hansda 2021). To rehabilitate Horo as both a social reality and as anthropological provocation, Pashupati sought to decouple the oppositional nature of the Horo-Diku phrase.

In reconstituting the Horo-Mitan term, he aimed to realign the Horo (the Human) or, more accurately, Hor-Hoponko (Our Humanity), with an affirmative worldview. He identified this as characterising the integrative and inclusive value systems of eastern India's Adivasi populations (see Sudeshna Dutta 2019; Kumar 2014), and this is what he self-identified with. Importantly, for Pashupati, the history of antagonism that is referred to in the Horo-Diku formulation (see testimony of Babulal Murmu Adivasi in 'Hul Sengel'), covers up a longer and socially inclusive history—of togetherness, familial coexistence, community exogamy, linguistic change and cultural innovation—that focused on the Adivasi people but that crucially also involved their agrarian neighbours, such as the Mahatos, to the extent that these adjunct groups could see themselves as part and parcel of the region's inclusive, positive-minded and collective (rather than binary, negatively inflected and fractured) Adivasi-hood (Mahato 1997; 2000; 2003). In this light, Pashupati wanted to advance the Horo-Mitan phenomenon, with a view to providing a more accurate and more rounded understanding of Horo: as 'us all', in the manner of Hor-Hoponko (rather than as 'us versus them'). This is because the human values that were at the heart of this place-specific Adivasi democracy and humanism, and its emergence over the centuries, are readily forgotten when the conditions of being 'human' (Horo) are either poorly defined by others, or else brought into being as a response to external threats (that is to say as Horo versus Diku).

In reading other work by Pashupati, it is clear that he was also very responsive to the historical processes through which different facets of India's 'caste' society could oppress or silence the Horo-Mitan or Adivasi cultural heritage (Mahato 2000). As with many other anthropologists and Humanities exponents in India, the provocations came thick and fast from Pashupati. What emerged in his academic writings, therefore, was a commitment to Humanity, to Adivasi-hood, and to anthropology via the vexed idea of Horo, and the related apprehensions (ancient and modern) around being Adivasi or, more pertinently, non-Adivasi. In his search for a form of socially responsive academic expression, which could properly represent and embody human or Horo values, he arrived at Horo-Mitan. It is in line with this pacific reasoning that one can productively broach the political philosophy of being 'non-Adivasi'. As exponents of methodological and cultural pluralism, we will need to discern, and then combine and bring into a productive relation, the many different facets of our 'humanities' selves that pertain to various communities at different times. In a way, this will enable practitioners not only to develop different facets and prospects of responsibility, but also to ensure that these become operative in collective and 'higher' educational programmes.

Part Seven: The voices of human dignity and recognition

In view of our previous engagements with Adivasi humanism, and the educational prospects that these offer to socially conscious non-Adivasis, this part explores different articulations of 'human dignity' (see Kolnai 1976; Mascimento and Lutz-Bachmann 2017), emphasising how and why they resonate in respect of Adivasi Studies in modern India. The main contention is that human dignity featured in early and overtly 'national' responses to issues of Adivasi or tribal 'backwardness' and that, as such, it requires some special analytical attention. It can also become a more integral feature of Adivasi Studies, if it is approached via forms of conceptual and cultural pluralism. The presence of human dignity in historic domains of Adivasi-hood is a difficult phenomena to grasp: not that it was not present, just that its qualities are contested and its role in the development of state/citizen relations is lesser known. One could contend that the pivotal conceptualisation of an Adivasi citizenry in modern India—as Scheduled Tribes—was premised on the search for social justice and social integration (see Ambagudia 2011), but not Adivasi autonomy. The introduction of human dignity into all of those social, political, legal, cultural, moral and educational realms pertaining to Adivasis in modern India was enabled to a large extent by (pro-Adivasi) non-Adivasi activists. As a term, 'non-Adivasi' is neither eloquent nor a particularly focused descriptor. It does, however, indicate a complex domain of socio-political action and philosophy, especially when considered in terms of Adivasi self-perception and problems of cross-cultural representation (see Sangeeta Dasgupta 2018;

Rycroft 2014a). So, the next provocation involves the search for human dignity and its complex relation to India's Adivasis, as well as to an array of evolving socio-political relationships that involve Adivasis as 'tribal' citizens.

The complexity of the relation is primarily due to the co-presence, in human rights discourses in India, of issues of human dignity (and humanism) and cultural recognition (and cultural pluralism). This way of thinking about identity and the imperatives of cultural translation is inspired both by the political effects of Adivasi assertions in India, and by the intellectual legacies of a number of Gandhian-era thinkers and activists. Of these, G. C. Sondhi (a Congress leader and social activist) and Upendra Maharathi (a Congress visual artist) merit particular attention. Sondhi, for example, sought to introduce Gandhian concepts like Swaraj (self-rule) into the modern social fabric, as a means to reanimate the pre-colonial dignity of Adivasi peoples and cultures, which Upendra Maharathi would aim to translate into visual form (see Part Eight). This dignity-centred ethos was summarised by one of Sondhi's close pro-Adivasi associates, J. C. Hayward, who was a prominent figure in the early years of the Adivasi Sabha and was a member of the Adivasi Sabha Deputation to the Prime Minister of Bihar in 1939: 'There was a time when the Mundas called Jharkhand their own, but today they are fallen. They are called backward and primitive, but with all this they are descendants of glorious ancestors. Today they live in abject poverty and are downtrodden. But the coming of Swaraj may once again restore them to happiness and prosperity' (Hayward 1940, 16). It was as a combination of Adivasis and 'non-Adivasis', therefore, that the Adivasi Sabha attempted during the mid-twentieth century to define spaces of 'inter' citizenship: wherein the political and cultural value-systems of Adivasis and non-Adivasis could become better aligned (Pankaj 2017, 35). Their integrationist work, therefore, came with its own set of representational dilemmas and limitations: in other words, whenever these were applied there was no guarantee that these would be free from either positive or negative stereotyping. As non-Adivasis, the Congress activists learnt of Adivasi perspectives through a combination of Adivasi and non-Adivasi representations. As noted by the early Adivasi social reformer, Jaipal Singh Munda:

> The Adibasi [sic] Sabha stands primarily for the moral and material advancement of Chota Nagpur and the Santhal Parganas, for the economic and political freedom of the Aboriginal Tracts ... Our Organisation is in full harmony with the principles of the Indian National Congress ... We shall fight unto death for our religious, cultural, linguistic and other rights. We must have a place of honour in the national life of India. (Munda 1939)

As supporters of this sense of Adivasi citizenship, the non-Adivasi activists embarked in different ways on a process of national integration that sought to create for Adivasis more responsive political, legal, scholarly and ethical frameworks, through which a new kind of comparative and emotionally literate citizenship could emerge. The effects and legacies and these frameworks are often overlooked in Adivasi Studies, meaning that an enhanced sense of self-reflexivity amongst exponents of Adivasi Studies has recently been called for (see Sangeeta Dasgupta 2018). These frameworks were created amidst a complex array of culture-specific (national), humanist (international), and emergent (hybrid) philosophies and ideals, focused on human dignity and the historic dignity of Adivasis. Their creators responded to the possibility of identifying and connecting multiple registers of national and sub-national citizenship, as a means to realise the national prospect of inter-citizenship that facilitated a shared humanity and, through their constitutional safeguarding, specific social and political (i.e. minority) rights. In these areas of dialogue, social transformation, and political solidarity, a new forward-looking yet 'negative' subjectivity evolved: that of the (pro-Adivasi) non-Adivasi.

In the pre-independence phase, this subjectivity involved social philosophers, such as Brajendranath Seal, Sarat Chandra Roy, and Radhakamal Mukerjee, who sought to engage different kinds of social, legal, political, and educational responsibilities in a collective effort to protect and sustain the interests, as well as the emerging citizenship rights, of Adivasi communities across different parts of India (Rycroft 2012b). Their work had a clear impact on the formation and later utility of anthropology and sociology during and after India's independence (see Rycroft 2012; 2015a). This era of decolonisation gave rise to a host of new institutions and ways of thinking that sought to make the diverse identities and claims of Adivasis meaningful and relevant to the nation at large. Historians and sociologists are steadily coming to terms with the representational, linguistic, and ethical dynamics of such frameworks, and the spaces of minority citizenship that they nurtured. My own sense is that there is real scope for further critical and reflexive work to ensue: in respect of the (pro-Adivasi) non-Adivasi demography that now characterises the field of Adivasi Studies, and the broader socio-cultural complexities that characterised the emergence of human dignity in modern India. My own perspective attempts to focus on the emergence of human dignity as a pre-condition for Adivasi 'inter' citizenship.

In view of my previous discussions, it will come as no surprise to readers to note that it is the historic characterisation, by non-Adivasis of India's Adivasis as comprising a 'submerged' humanity (Bijoy 1993), that lends itself to this kind of reappraisal. If submergence is the negation (i.e. the negative form) of emergence, then both sides (i.e. positive and negative) of emergence need to be called into question, with a view to identifying and analysing their conceptual value and their social production. To address the emergence of human dignity in this manner is to acknowledge that the emergence in question is not a one-way phenomenon, for example from indignity to dignity. Indeed, I use the term emergence with its negative corollary (i.e. submergence) equally in view. This is a difficult but necessary task, wherein the socio-political conditions behind the use of terms like 'submerged' or 'backward' require reconsideration. Whilst the key historical evidence here pertains to the 1930s and 1940s—and the heightened authority and influence of the Indian National Congress—it is intended that the analysis has contemporary decolonial resonance. Whilst this pre-independence authority sought to carry forward new constitutional and moral priorities, its prescriptive formulations of Adivasi identity did not enable a fuller Adivasi social consciousness to emerge, either then or in the decades since independence. This is why we need to remain attentive to the issue of submergence.

My own work on these kinds of issues has evolved out of my much earlier interest in the relationship between art, history, and anthropology in India, as eloquently and provocatively summarised by Sandip Luis in his analysis of the artistic connection between Jagdish Swaminathan and Jangarh Singh Shyam (Luis 2019). In many ways, the aesthetic and institutional intimacy these two luminaries of India's art world provides a compelling portal through which to explore issues concerning (pro-Adivasi) non-Adivasi subjectivity. Swaminathan's pro-Adivasi approach generated—via its emphasis on cultural translation and mutuality—important insights concerning Adivasi humanity and heritage. These can be taken as evidence of an underlying affinity between Swaminathan and Jangarh, whose identity as a Pardhan Gond (Adivasi) artist was crucial to Swaminathan's vision. Swaminathan's intercultural effort was predicated on a search for social justice through cultural transformation, in view of the structural marginalisation of Adivasis and the ongoing need to confront this, via new forms of creativity and communication. Whilst the economic fortunes of many exponents of the 'Jangarh Kalam' (that is, Jangarh-inspired art forms) testify to the longevity and value of Swaminathan's intervention, the broader experience of being Adivasi in India is not so positive (Das 2017). Indeed Jangarh's suicide may be taken as symptomatic of a much broader structural malaise. This is evident in the many environmental, educational, and politico-economic injustices and pressures that impact on the everyday lives of many poor, displaced, and non-urban Adivasi citizens (see Singh 2013; Nilsen 2019).

Reconnecting with issues of human dignity and human responsibility is, and should remain, an enriching yet difficult task. It could bring the work of all exponents of Adivasi Studies into a new kind of collectivity: to set in motion a more transformative and philosophical sense of why and how our academic, social, and ideational works might proceed in tandem, not only with one another, but also with the shifting terrains of Adivasi citizenship and global justice (see Bandhu and Jacob 2019). On this point, one might want to note that the UN's Agenda 2030 for the Implementation of the Sustainable Development Goals was originally entitled the Road to Dignity by 2030 (United Nations 2014). Interestingly, the Five Principles that harness the social, environmental and economic justice agendas of the 2030 Agenda point to the proposition that some sections of the global population are routinely denied human dignity or, put differently, are 'left behind' due to human rights abuses, and a lack of access to water, welfare, healthcare, and education (Weber 2017). These concerns, to my mind, offer important entry points into issues of colonial legacies and neo-colonial human relations, for the Indian nation-state rarely concedes to Adivasis the opportunity to represent themselves, whether in national and international domains, and whether as members of a national confederation or as a part of a transnational 'indigenous' collective (see Niezen 2003; Rycroft 2011).

The UN's guidance to governments and civil society organisations to Leave No One Behind attempts to ensure that vulnerable, including 'Indigenous', populations are not excluded from the developmental, technological, and educational provisions that are put in place in an effort ostensibly to modernise and empower societies worldwide (Yap and Watene 2019). The idea of human dignity can take on an instrumental as well as an ethical quality, and this requires some unpacking, especially if one takes seriously the 'resistance' to development agendas, whether these agendas are communicated through the maxims of nation-building, multilateralism, or community inclusion (see Marglin 1990; Dutta 2020). In contemporary times, this takes us into difficult arenas of (non) recognition, and the (non) participation of minorities in 'dominant' institutions and economies, such as Higher Education, even if India has recently appointed a Santal bureaucrat as its first ever 'tribal' President (see Basu Ray Chaudhury 2009; Pannikar and Bhaskaran Nair 2011). It is heartening to see that scholars such as Neville Panthaki have gone further, by raising the possibility for a convergence between Adivasi Studies and critical pedagogy (Panthaki 2016). We are also pleased to see the convergence of Indian and international approaches to indigeneity in arenas such as the *Journal of Adivasi and Indigenous Studies.*

As scholars familiar with Adivasi Studies will note, a positive part of 'becoming Adivasi' pertains to the multiple and multidimensional forms of Adivasi learning, self-representation, reflection, and resistance that enable a sense of freedom to coexist with a sense of belonging: whether within, aside, or against the political, educational, and economic mainstreams of India. It is through these kinds of positive experiences that human dignity literally starts to make more sense as a concept, whether for Adivasis or for non-Adivasis drawn in different ways into Adivasi spaces of history, peace, democracy, citizenship, and wellbeing. A critique should be developed that draws attention to the relative absence both of Adivasi experiences and sense-making processes, in studies of human dignity and human rights at large, and human dignity, in appreciations and representations of Adivasi pasts and futures. As a means to engender this kind of collective reappraisal, which might in time enable these relative absences to be questioned and perhaps resolved, contributors to our Pluralist Pedagogy Movement might do worse than focusing on the Adivasi Humanities, and what it means for the Humanities in India to translate into the Adivasi Humanities, and vice versa. The Adivasi Humanities would need to be able to embrace both the big picture and the contextual nature of its articulation, via different kinds of Adivasi, tribal and intercultural experience. As such, it might over time be possible for exponents to envision a vast horizon of collective action that enables the emergence of human dignity at the heart of both Adivasi-related scholarship/education and Adivasi citizenship/democracy. This is what I aim to bring into focus, through the combination of the voices of recognition, responsibility and dignity.

Part Eight: The voices of rights and the anti-colonial nation

As previously intimated, a good number of philosophies of human dignity exist. This next provocation is inspired equally by the work of Marcus Duwell and Walter Mignolo, and their ideas to envisage future human convergences along multiple lines of human dignity. Both of these writers have brought the question of human dignity centrally into their work, but to different ends (Duwell 2014; Mignolo 2006). For Mignolo, human dignity is an unwritten, largely unheard, and non-instrumental idea that might help us to ascertain a decolonial humanity in the future. For Duwell, human dignity is a central pillar of human rights education and related forms of global governance. Duwell's main task is to question whether human dignity is the means to achieve human rights, or whether the reverse holds true: that human dignity is achieved through human rights. As perhaps both propositions are true, depending on contexts, cultures and circumstances, Duwell argues that different versions, horizons and philosophies of human dignity are in operation concurrently. In this domain of cultural difference, advocates sometimes speak in conversation with each other, yet they sometimes speak against or across each other. I would encourage exponents of Adivasi Studies to reflect on this key point.

Duwell's idea is to understand the global diversity of the human dignity field, and the significance of this diversity to human rights education. As such, human dignity anticipates a combination of anthropological (or culture-specific) as well as more integrative and universal representations of human values. As evaluated by Aggarwal (2015), such concerns require reassessment in the context of modern India, given the predominance of human dignity—and the 'right to rights', especially for marginal and vulnerable groups—in India's Constitution. As such, human dignity can be taken forward as a pluralistic yet pivotal concept that underwrites Adivasi and subaltern claims on citizenship. Just as Duwell and Mignolo arrive at the meaning and significance of human dignity differently, so in all probability we understand human dignity in accordance with a varied and perhaps rather open-ended sense of what it might mean (see Mattson and Clark 2011; Gier 2010; Spiegelberg 1971): whether as human rights and their violation; as our own and others' social responsibilities; or—in the Gandhian idiom of virtuous humility—as the ethical reach of duties and devotion. As always with human dignity, we are left pondering difficult questions, such as: is your understanding of human dignity comparable with mine and, if so, to what extent? And: how have our ideas of human dignity arisen, and what effect do they have on social, philosophical, and educational activism, especially in view of Adivasi and Indigenous Studies? My point is to develop a more focused engagement with human dignity, so that these kinds of questions become answerable, and so that we become better equipped to ascertain our own involvement in variously moral, social, political, and pedagogic decisions and judgements, with a view potentially to making higher education and the UN's Agenda 2030 more receptive to the conceptual richness and educational power of human dignity.

As Aggarwal (2015, 8) notes, exclusion or marginalisation from sites and processes of political, economic, educational, social, legal, and cultural participation amounts to structural discrimination or, in a word, indignity. A good reason to call all this into question, especially when we are thinking through different textures of Adivasi experience, is due to the tendency to couple human dignity to human rights discourse. Whilst this may end up being crucial to a full account of human dignity and its potential flourishing in modern India, it is a little problematic because it leads us into an already 'emerged', that is, defined and (to a degree) functioning, space of Adivasi citizenship and rights that broach Adivasi interests and identities within the preordained frameworks of Scheduled Tribes and Scheduled Areas. Might it not be more suitable—that is, value-congruent, especially in the context of an evolving sphere of Adivasi Studies that proffers new kinds of intellectual and epistemological inclusion and diversity—to try to ascertain the idea of human dignity in view of overtly Adivasi axioms, experiences, and worldviews? There could be educational and ethical benefits in not privileging historical assumptions, whether about Adivasis or human dignity, even when these feature seemingly helpful and progressive notions, such as human rights.

An anti-colonial and integrative ethos is needed to define both the particularity of Adivasi social consciousness and the areas of value-congruency between national and sub-national citizenship. The proto-constitutional debates involving the Indian National Congress, around 'racial' minorities and protected or Excluded Areas in the 1930s, delineated key issues pertaining to such phenomena as integration, assimilation, cultural transition and cultural translation (Rycroft 2012; 2014b; 2017; 2017a). Whilst the Tribal Studies approach might gloss over these phenomena, an Adivasi Studies approach would aim to reassess them, in view for example of their relevance to contemporary Adivasi (inter) citizenship. Whilst we are not arguing necessarily for a new Constitution or a new Republic, we are suggesting that other sites—beyond the Constitution—should be prioritised by those attempting to re-evaluate the presence/absence of human dignity in Adivasi contexts. This is because Adivasis did not write the Constitution. Rather, it was written for them and for others at a time when considerations of Adivasi agency, humanism, rights, philosophy, heritage, identity and knowledge were in the process of evolving, but were noticeably under-nourished by India's political and educational leaders. This is why it may prove to be productive, for Higher Educational Institutions to support Basu Ray Chaudhury's idea (2009) to construct a new 'Indian Charter' for minority rights.

The aforementioned criteria for being human and attaining citizenship were for the most part created for, and by, non-Adivasi interests and norms. These interests, and their introduction and management in post-colonial India, reflect the ambiguous and uneven presence of human dignity in modern India. It is disheartening to note that even though they acknowledge the presence of Adivasi citizenship and heritage, they did not enable Adivasis to contribute directly or en masse either to the issues or the futures at hand. We can earmark this non-emergent or 'submerged' phenomenon within a broader arena: the dignity deficit. So, the effects of both emergent and submerged phenomena need to be somehow addressed together, but this is a difficult task to pursue, as one's perception and apprehension of the overall terrain is likely to be skewed either in favour of emergence and optimism, or else submergence and realism. To some extent to reach a consensus, on the extent and efficacy of either emergence or submergence, is less of a priority than to acknowledge that emergence and submergence coexist circumstantially, and will continue to do so for as long as questions of 'Adivasi humanity' and human dignity are muted, marginalised, or misappropriated. One can therefore conceptualise an understanding of Adivasi emergence/submergence: in terms that involve human dignity; that articulate emergence and submergence in manifold and interestingly interconnected ways; and that accord with the variously legal, political, ethical, social, aesthetic, or scholarly norms of the day.

Of course, for human dignity to realise its potential as either a cosmopolitan or a context-specific 'ideal', it has to first emerge, both in a literal and in an analytical sense. Early non-Adivasi exponents of Indian anthropology, such as Sarat Chandra Roy, focused not only on the more vulnerable and impoverished Adivasi societies in India, but also on the more powerful representatives of Adivasi culture and heritage, whose participation in the making of the modern constitution was rather indirect but who, like the infamous Birsa Munda, had a clear sense of Adivasi freedom (Rycroft 2016). There is a rare pencil drawing, now in the Patna Museum, that depicts Birsa Munda: it is an image that aims to translate a colonialist photograph of Birsa as a captive rebel into an embodiment of both Munda (Adivasi) and national heritage. It is a historic visual manifestation of the idea of Adivasi (inter) citizenship that I have been discussing. It is by the non-Adivasi visual artist Upendra Maharathi who, as a practitioner of modern 'heritage' art, had become expert in creating an iconography that chimed with commonplace ideas of national idealism. It was commissioned by the Indian National Congress in preparation for its Ramgarh conference in 1940, and was thought to have entered Gandhi's private collection at that time. Maharathi was also involved in designing and constructing the temporary pavilions for the Congress (Rycroft 2016; National Gallery of Modern Art 2021). In this image, Birsa's political and human dignity is recast, with a view to providing viewers with an opportunity to apprehend not only (a) his own movement for enhanced autonomy amongst Munda Adivasis, but also (b) the broader idea of Adivasi-hood, or long-term indigeneity in the region of Jharkhand (formerly Southern Bihar). As a Congress product, it also affirmed the emergent idea of anti-colonial or national decolonisation. As a representative of Munda claims of Adivasi self-rule in the late nineteenth century, Birsa's political identity also assumed posthumous importance. By the early twentieth century, and in the years that followed his death in Ranchi prison, he still retained political influence, as is seen in the formation of the Chota Nagpur Tenancy Act (CNTA), which itself legitimated the idea of Excluded and Partially Excluded Areas that would later inform Congress policy on Scheduled Areas.

The image is impressive, particularly in its almost effortless capacity to resurrect Birsa from the colonial archive as an embodiment of human dignity: to introduce the possibility both of an embodied and real, but also somehow higher or transcendent relation with viewers. We know from administrative and anthropological records that in the years preceding his Ulgulan (or rebellion) Birsa had won the support of many Munda villagers on account of his prophetic and healing qualities. He developed a following of devotees, who became known as Birsaites and who were largely responsible for the political agitations that followed Birsa's initial capture and imprisonment in the mid-1890s. They saw in Birsa a multidimensional prospect, or someone who could exceed the regular limitations of lived human existence, to the extent that he could, by his semi-divine powers, create a properly dignified existence for them. As with other Adivasi memorials, our experiencing of human dignity here is truly vexed: why should the Birsaites have had to fight for their ancestral rights? Can any political or anthropological interventions, such as the CNTA, ever offset the traumas associated with the self-sacrifice of the Birsaites? Why do we see Birsa and not them? In view of his capacity to take onboard multiple political and religious influences, Birsa has since earned the epithet, amongst others, of Gandhi-before-Gandhi. But is this gesture, of synchronising Birsa's legacy with India's father of human dignity, helpful? Has anyone claimed Gandhi to be Birsa-after-Birsa?

Putting that thought on hold, we should consider what would have been an intriguing moment: the moment when Gandhi, presiding over the Ramgarh Congress, himself took Birsa *darsana*: to come to understand himself, the world, and the interrelation, even briefly, through Birsa's eyes, and as an extension of Birsa's social consciousness. As such, he would have assumed an important intersubjectivity, connecting him—as a devotee of freedom, of India, and of devotion—directly to Birsa's own devotees: the Birsaites. That an image such as this could create such synergy and devotional empathy might impress on us the need to both exist with, but also to transcend, the social categories that marked Birsa an Adivasi and Gandhi a non-Adivasi. We can therefore re-view the image by Maharathi to consider how the image spoke to an emergent national culture that sought to reconnect the state and the people, or put another way the Congress and the marginal groups, such as the Mundas. The image re-translates Birsa into the kind of space created for him by his followers: as prophet or leader worthy of respect and devotion. The image therefore provides a portal into an anti-colonial Congress imaginary, which sought to decolonise the relationship between Adivasis and non-Adivasis, as well as between India and the world. As such, it presented Birsa in the way that he thought of himself: as the embodiment of a long line of shared experience and oppressed dignity, and as the creative mind behind the emergence of a free future.

To me, the image also presents an opportunity to go one stage further: to reimagine the Birsaites themselves as devotees of Birsa. They are invoked as the 'absent' presence that liberates the colonial gaze, and that enables the devotional qualities of the image, and the idea of freedom, to rise simultaneously to the surface. To ascertain this sense of presence is important if we are to render Birsaism relevant to lost and recovered sites of human dignity. If we are to speak of the Fifth Schedule, we must be willing to do so in a way that not only accounts for Adivasi resistance but also creates space for the ecological, ancestral and political rights of Adivasis to emerge and coexist. In this light, we are confronted with a very ambiguous image that speaks of difficult relationships, difficult identities, difficult times, difficult futures, and violated, submerged ideals. If Birsa is to be seen as an iconic figure, with a multidimensional presence, what are we to make of the Birsaites' devotional agency now? Should it be located simply as an extension of and adherence to the ethos of Birsa, or might it also pertain to the broader idea and heritage of Bhakti (devotion) that was deeply encoded into the Gandhian principles of Swadeshi (self-reliance), Swaraj (self-rule), and Satyagraha (truth-force)? I would contend that we may benefit by taking stock of these emergent and difficult questions, and what they mean for us and for future generations, whether as specific pointers concerning presence and absence, or as part and parcel of more institutionalised terrains of human dignity, ecological wisdom and Adivasi citizenship.

In this light, the textual representation of Birsa by the Congress leader G. C. Sondhi is quite helpful. Just as Birsa was the key thinker of the Ulgulan, so Sondhi assumed a pivotal role in the production and interpretation of the Ramgarh Congress session. His fascination with Birsa and what he stood for, both literally at the time of the Ulgulan (i.e. Adivasi freedom) and metaphorically in the era after the Ulgulan (that is, Adivasi rights), merits a short enquiry as it connects with a number of important features in the national recognition of Adivasi identity: namely (i) 'Indian' anthropology, via the work of Roy; (ii) the political effects of the Ulgulan, via the CNTA; and (iii) the social responsibilities of the Congress, to recognise and redress structural and social inequalities in ways that could sustain Adivasi citizenship and humanity, if not necessarily Adivasi freedom and self-determination. As editor of the Congress Commemoration Volume, Sondhi's heritage-oriented views on different facets of the national decolonisation movement, such as democracy, integration, and idealism, are clear (Sondhi 1948). Whilst this volume does not 'commemorate' the Adivasis at all, it does provide a broader context through which to appraise the Congress' reception of Birsa Munda and his legacy, as exemplified in their naming of the Birsa Munda gate at the Ramgarh Congress session, and Sondhi's focus on Birsa Munda in the Ramgarh Congress Souvenir (Sondhi 1940). In his short tract on 'Birsa Bhagwan: Rebel Prophet of Adibasis [sic]', Sondhi provides a textual commentary on the social and political history of Jharkhand, which parallels and enriches Maharathi's contemporary visualisation of Birsa and his accompanying re-embodiment of Birsaism. The article includes a pen drawing of the familiar portrait of Birsa-as-captive that Maharathi used as his own source image. It is also illustrated with a typical Jharkhandi scene, namely the 'Santal [Adivasi] Dance' by Rani Chanda, which echoed—in its sensitivity to the lived environment of Adivasis—both contemporary works done by members of the Santiniketan School of visual arts, and translated Adivasi songs in the souvenir.

Interestingly, Sondhi's commentary (1940, 88) also emphasised his own experience of being imprisoned at Ranchi Jail, the site of Birsa's captivity and eventual demise. The article then focuses on Birsa's identity as a 'product of historical forces' (1940, 89), namely anticolonial insurrections and ongoing proletariat discontent, as well as Birsa's transition from being a 'Socio religious teacher' to becoming, in the eyes of his followers, 'the father of the world' or Dharti Aba (Sondhi 1940, 89). For Sondhi, the fact that Birsa was able to develop and sustain a 'high purpose and deep influence' (Sondhi 1940, 90) amongst different classes and sects of Mundas meant that he should be considered as an equal to other national freedom fighters, despite the quick and brutal suppression of the Ulgulan. Of note, in respect of contemporary discussions of Adivasi emergence and submergence, is Sondhi's willingness to identify in the resilience of Birsa and amongst the Adivasis of the Jharkhand region both a historical awareness and a future-minded socio-political consciousness. Sondhi could thus explore how Munda spirituality and heritage might equate, in the eyes of the Congress, to India's search for national/human dignity. This notion is elaborated more fully in Sondhi's Commemorative volume of 1948, under the auspices of India's Charter for Freedom. It may be quoted at length:

> This Constitutional Assembly declares its firm and solemn resolve to proclaim India as an Independent Sovereign Republic and to draw up for her future governance a Constitution ... Wherein all power and authority of the Sovereign Independent India, its constituent parts and organs of government, are derived from the people, and wherein shall be guaranteed and secured to all people of India justice social, economic, and political ... Wherein adequate safeguards shall be provided for minorities, and for backward and tribal areas ... [So that] This ancient land attains its rightful and honoured place in the world, and makes its full and willing contribution to the promotion of world peace and the welfare of mankind. (Sondhi 1948, 411)

The point is to highlight how and why the architects of this dignity-centric national future were aware of Birsa Munda, to the extent that they deemed Birsaism—that is, the belief that Birsa's ideals, presence, and memory should live on—to become more relevant to the future of India and therefore operative in the evolution of (Adivasi) humanity. This quotation helps us to understand the various educational, legal, administrative, moral and environmental dimensions of Adivasi-oriented social responsibility. But when it comes to Adivasi struggles, in accordance with whose terms or frames of reference might one actually be prepared to take-the-oath, if at all?

Conclusion

As an experiment in methodological pluralism, this text has explored a number of approaches to the salient historical and contemporary dimensions of academic/intellectual and intercultural social responsibility. There are, of course, numerous other issues and perspectives that readers may want to introduce within this evolving discourse in due time. Each of these perspectives will need to be rendered in accordance with their specific personal and professional, as well as disciplinary and institutional, resonance. In communicating and reflecting upon such experiences, a shared discourse (complete with relevant discursive strategies) may emerge, and it will be in accordance with this communicative and pedagogical endeavour that 'patterns of value and responsibility' may start to accrue future significance. It is in line with this articulated sense of responsibility that the future of our disciplines, and the future of related areas of knowledge, thought, action, professionalism, and ethics may prosper.

As the 'Humanities in India' collective, we have sought to link and when necessary also to delink 'academic' social responsibility from institutional level responsibilities, which are also steadily evolving as part and parcel of the international discourse of University Social Responsibility. This is a formal discourse that broaches university-level commitments to key challenges, such as social justice, social inclusion, and sustainability. Not all academics, especially anthropologists, and other Humanities exponents who are wary of aligning themselves too closely to institutionalised norms, are dialled into university-level policies and practices. This means that the process of aligning 'academic' social responsibility work to USR agendas will, in part, need to become strategic, given the search for a productive and sustainable balance between institutional visibility, recognition and impact, and disciplinary specificity, social ethics and human/intellectual freedoms. One of the premises of transversal and dialogic practice is that one can use the process of intra-institutional and inter-institutional dialogue to develop and enhance the case for either (i) a better alignment of individual and collective engagements of social responsibility, and vice versa, or (ii) spaces of mutual recognition, wherein the specific prospects of and for 'academic' social responsibility might become better known and better understood by those involved in university-level governance. Given these limitations, the overall usefulness of either the 'Humanities' (as a plethora of disciplines) or the 'humanities' (as the cross-cultural interpretation of becoming human) may be invoked. In identifying as either Humanities or 'humanities' exponents, practitioners must become better equipped to develop dialogues and exchanges, including translations, that will help everyone to reconstruct pluralistic architectonics of diversity and inclusion. It is a non-stop process.

In addressing the 'voices' of pluralism, we are compelled to think in terms of interdependence and to address this as a characteristic of value-congruence and dialogue. Interdependence is not singularly a quality of the Humanities, or even of academia at large, even if the inherent pluralism of the Humanities is nurtured by, and responsible for, this shared quality. Interdependence is a phenomenon that exists and thrives at the cusp of the more singular facets of learning, knowledge-creation, and social transformation. Whilst it is sometimes important to recognise the particular power, agency and value of these aforementioned facets, it is equally important also to consider their co-creation, co-incidence, and co-development. I have over recent years become interested in understanding how and why certain forms of 'Indian' anthropology were envisaged and embodied by different academicians before, during, and after India's independence. Just as advocates of the UN's Agenda 2030 advocate strategies and processes that address more than one goal or target, so dialogical learning responds to the mutual significance of diverse value systems, congruent and complex voices, and multi-tiered responsibilities. All 'Humanities' teachers and learners, may benefit from cultivating an enhanced responsiveness to the principles, politics and philosophies—whether short-term or long-term, direct or indirect, indigenous or non-indigenous—that animate our academic practices. It is in this multidimensional space, of thought, action, knowledge, understanding, experience, responsibility, humanity, and co-presence, that the real value of the 'humanities' is brought into existence. It is here that we can reflect on our 'discursive being' and then make these reflections significant to each other.

References

Aggarwal, Komila. 2015. *Right to Human Dignity: A Critical Study with Special Reference to the Marginalised Section in India* (PhD Dissertation). Jammu: University of Jammu.

Agrawal, Suren and J. C. Aggarwal. 1991. *Educational and Social Uplift of Backward Classes, at what cost and how? Mandal Commission and After*. New Delhi: Concept Publishing.

Ambagudia, Jagannath. 2011. 'Scheduled Tribes and the Politics of Inclusion in India.' *Asian Social Work and Policy Review* 5: 33–43.

Acharya, Indranil. 2017. 'Discourse of Marginality and the Indigenous Literature of Australia and India: A Study.' *Middle Flight* 6: 131–41.

Asiatic Society. 2019. 'Translating Bodo Short Stories: A Seminar-Workshop.' Held in conjunction with 'RUSA 2.0 Programme on Archiving and Translating Indigenous and Marginalised Traditions.' 21–25 October. Kolkata: Collaboration with CENTIL (Jadavpur University) and 'Humanities in India Partnership Programme' (UEA).

Avest, Ina ter, and Cok Bakkar. 2020. 'Disruptive moments and normative professionalism: An exploration of the (im)possibilities of a provocative pedagogy to stimulate the development of normative professionalism.' In *Scholarly Engagement and Decolonisation: Views from South Africa, The Netherlands and the United States*, edited by Maurice Crul, et al, 139–62. Stellenbosch: African Sun Media.

Ban, Ki-moon. 2010. 'The United Nations Academic Impact', *UN Chronicle* XLVII(3). https://unchronicle.org.un/issue/what-united-nations-academic-impact.

Bandhu, Pranjali and T. G. Jacob. 2019. *Encountering the Adivasi Question*. Delhi: Studera Press.

Banerjee, Prathama. 2006. *Politics of Time: 'Primitives' and History-writing in a Colonial Society*. New Delhi: Oxford University Press.

Basu Ray Chaudhury, Sabyasachi. 2009. 'An Indian Charter for Minority Rights.' In *State of Justice in India: Issues of Social Justice*, edited by R. Samaddar, 334–70. New Delhi: Sage.

Bellier, Irene. 2010. 'Scales of Governance: The UN and Indigenous Peoples (SOGIP).' Consultation event held in December 2010. New Delhi: Indian Centre for Social Science Research.

Berman, Sheldon and Phyllis La Farge. 1993. *Promising Practices in Teaching Social Responsibility*. Albany: State University of New York Press.

Beverley, John. 1998. 'Theses on Subalternity, Representation, and Hegemony.' *Postcolonial Studies* 1(3): 305–319.

Biehl, Joao, et al, 2007. 'Introduction: Rethinking Subjectivity.' In *Subjectivity: Ethnographic Investigations*, edited by Joao Biehl, et al, 1–24. Berkeley: University of California Press.

Bijoy, C. R. 1993. 'Emergence of the Submerged: Indigenous People at UN.' *Economic and Political Weekly* 26 June, 1357–60.

Bilimoria, Purushottama, ed. 2017. *History of Indian Philosophy*. Abingdon: Routledge.

Boone, Katie. 2020. 'Achieving SDGs through Academic Diplomacy.' In *University Social Responsibility: From Dialogue to Implementation*, edited by Daniel Rycroft et al, 36–37. Norwich: UEA (India Dialogue).

Bradley-Birt, F. B. 1905. *The Story of an Indian Upland*. London: Smith, Elder, and Co.

Braidotti, Rosa and Paul Gilroy. 2016. 'Introduction.' In *Conflicting Humanities*, edited by Rosa Braidotti and Paul Gilroy, 1–8. London: Bloomsbury.

Chakrabarty, Dipesh. 2004. 'Minority Histories, Subaltern Pasts.' In *Postcolonial Passages: Contemporary History writing on India*, edited by Saurabh Dube, 229–42. New Delhi: Oxford University Press.

Chambers, Ellie, ed. 2013. *Contemporary Themes in Humanities Higher Education*. Cham: Springer International.

Chandra, U. 2015. 'Towards Adivasi Studies: New Perspectives on 'Tribal' Margins of Modern India.' *Studies in History* 31(1): 122–27.

Chandramohan, Balasubramanyam and Daniel Rycroft. 2018. 'Academic Diplomacy, an Evolving Discipline.' *Diplomacy and Beyond: A Journal of Foreign Policy and National Affairs*, 13 November. https://diplomacybeyond.com/academic-diplomacy-an-evolving-discipline/.

Chatterji, Roma. 2004. 'Purulia Chho: Discursive Space and the Constitution of Culture.' In *Folklore, Public Sphere and Civil Society*, edited by M. D. Muthukumaraswamy and Molly Kaushal, 37–55. New Delhi: Indira Gandhi National Centre for the Arts.

Chelstrom, Eric. 2013. *Social Phenomenology: Husserl, Intersubjectivity, and Collective Intentionality*. Lanham: Lexington Books.

Cole, David and Joff Bradley, eds. 2018. *Principles of Transversality in Globalization and Education*. Singapore: Springer Nature.

Crowder, George. 2019. *The Problem of Value Pluralism: Isaiah Berlin and Beyond*. London: Routledge.

Crul, Maurice et al. 2020. 'Scholarly engagement and decolonisation.' In *Scholarly Engagement and Decolonisation: Views from South Africa, The Netherlands and the United States*, edited by Maurice Crul et al, 1–26. Stellenbosch: African Sun Media.

Das, Aurogeeta. 2017. *Jangarh Singh Shyam: The Enchanted Forest*. New Delhi: Roli Books.

Das, Samir Kumar. 2021. 'Peace as Power, Power of Peace.' In *Peace and Conflict Studies: Perspectives from South Asia*, edited by Anindya Jyoti Majumdar and Shibashis Chatterjee, Abingdon: Routledge.

Das, Samir Kumar and Ranabir Samaddar. 2009. *Ways of Power, Minorities, and Knowledge on Minorities: An Assessment of Research Policies and Practices*. Kolkata: Mahanirban Calcutta Research Group.

Dasgupta, Sangeeta. 2018. 'Adivasi studies: From a historian's perspective.' *History Compass*, e12486: 1–11.

Dasgupta, Sayantan. 2018. 'Rethinking Indian Literature, Reinventing Comparative Literature.' *Indian Literature* 62(4): 220–223.

Dasgupta, Sayantan, 'Dalit Writing in Bangla.' In *Subalternities in India and Latin America*, edited by Sonya Surabhi Gupta, 111–21. New Delhi: Routledge.

Dasgupta, Sayantan and Cecilia Rossi. 2021. 'What is Participatory Curriculum Development?' In *Dialogues on Decolonisation*, edited by Daniel Rycroft, 18–21. Norwich: UEA (India Dialogue).

Dasgupta, Sayantan and Daniel Rycroft. 2019. 'Academic Social Responsibility and the UN SDGs: Towards a New Humanities.' Final Report (Vice Chancellor's Global Challenges Research Fellowship programme). Norwich: UEA.

Department of Comparative Literature. 2019. 'RUSA 2.0 Visiting Fellowship on Archiving and Translating Indigenous and Marginalised Traditions.' Kolkata: Jadavpur University.

Deshpande, Satish. 2013. 'Introduction: Beyond Inclusion.' In *Beyond Inclusion: The Practices of Equal Access in Indian Higher Education*, edited by Satish Deshpande and Usma Zacharias, 1–12. London: Routledge.

Desmond, William. 2001. *Ethics and the Between*. Albany: State University of New York Press.

Devi, Mahasweta. 1995. *Imaginary Maps: Three Stories by Mahasweta Devi, Translated and Introduced by Gayatri Chakravorty Spivak*. Abingdon: Routledge.

Devy, Ganesh N. 2010. 'Inclusive Education: A View of Higher Education in India.' Public Lecture, 26 September. Bangalore: National Institute of Advanced Studies.

Devy, Ganesh N. 2013. 'Affirmative Action in Three Dream Institutions.' In *Beyond Inclusion: The Practices of Equal Access in Indian Higher Education*, edited by Satish Deshpande and Usma Zacharias, 72–94. London: Routledge.

Drees, Willem. 2021. *What are the Humanities for?* Cambridge: Cambridge University Press.

Dutta, Ishani. 2019. 'The 'Unity in Diversity' Problematic: A Critique of Comparative Literature in India.' *Sahitya* 8: 35–45.

Dutta, M. 2020. *Communication, Culture and Social Change: Meaning, Co-option and Resistance*. Cham: Palgrave Macmillan.

Dutta, Sudeshna. 2019. 'Understanding Adivasi existence in relation to the environmental identity and environmental heritage of Adivasi-Moolvasi communities of Jharkhand.' *Sahitya* 8: 113–30.

Duwell, Marcus. 2014. 'Human Dignity: concepts, discussions, philosophical perspectives.' In *The Cambridge Handbook of Human Dignity: Interdisciplinary Perspectives*, edited by M. Duwell et al, 23–49. Cambridge: Cambridge University Press.

Elliott, Mark. 2019. 'Decolonial Re-enactments? Facing and Retracing Colonial Histories in Collecting 'Another India'.' *Third Text* 33(4–5): 631–50.

Fassett, Deana and John Warren. 2006. *Critical Communication Pedagogy*. Thousand Oaks: Sage.

Freise, Matthias, ed. 2018. *Inspired by Bakhtin: Dialogic Methods in the Humanities*. Boston: Academic Studies Press.

Fry, Tony and Madina Tlostanova. 2021. *A New Political Imagination: Making the Case*. London: Routledge.

Gier, Nicholas. 2010. 'Confucius, Gandhi and the Aesthetics of Virtue.' *Asian Philosophy* 11(1): 41–54.

Godrej, Farah. 2009. 'Towards a Cosmopolitan Political Thought: The Hermeneutics of Interpreting the Other.' *Polity* 41(2): 135–65.

Goodale, Mark. 2018. 'Seventy-year-old views that remain contemporary.' *The UNESCO Courier* (October–December): 8–10.

Gozawa, Joanne, 2017. 'Intersubjectivity and Blended-Learning: Turning Learning Spaces to Wisdom's Place?' In *The Intersubjective Turn: Theoretical Approaches to Contemplative Learning and Inquiry across Disciplines*, edited by Olen Gunnlaugson et al, 59–82. Albany: State University of New York Press.

Gunnlaugson, Olen et al, eds. 2017. *The Intersubjective Turn: Theoretical Approaches to Contemplative Learning and Inquiry across Disciplines*. Albany: State University of New York Press.

Gupta, Malvika and Felix Padel. 2018. 'Confronting a pedagogy of assimilation: the evolution of large-scale schools for tribal children in India.' *Journal of the Anthropological Society of Oxford*, 10(1): 22–47.

Hansda, Naju. 2021. 'The Colonial Missionaries in Santal Parganas: In Search of Changing World of the Santals in Aftermath of Hul.' *Studies in Humanities and Social Sciences* 28(2): 24–41.

Hardison, Osborne. 1972. *Toward Freedom and Dignity: The Humanities and the Idea of Humanity*. Charles Village: John Hopkins Press.

Hayward, J. C. 1940. 'The Adivasis of Chhotanagpur.' In *Congress Souvenir: Ramgarh*, edited by G. C. Sondhi, 10–16. Calcutta: The Commercial Syndicate.

Heskovits, Melville. 2018. 'Individual rights and respect for all cultures.' *The UNESCO Courier* (October–December): 24–26.

Hok Ka Ma, Carol and Rajesh Tandon. 2014. 'Knowledge, Engagement and Higher Education in Asia and the Pacific.' In *Higher Education in the World 5*, edited by Global University Network for Innovation, 196–207. London: Palgrave Macmillan.

Humanities in India Partnerships Programme. 2017. *International Workshop on Curriculum Development: Full Report*. Norwich: UEA.

Humanities in India Partnerships Programme. 2018. *Report of International Workshop on Academic Social Responsibility (in association with Jadavpur University, Kolkata)*. Norwich: UEA.

Humanities in India Partnerships Programme. 2019. 'Jadavpur University Visit Report, June 2019.' Norwich: UEA.

Jezierska, Katarzyna and Leszek Koczanowicz, eds. 2015. *Democracy in Dialogue, Dialogue in Democracy: The Politics of Dialogue in Theory and Practice*. Farnham: Ashgate Publishing.

Jorgensen, Danny. 1989. *Participant Observation: A Methodology for Human Studies*. London: Sage Publications.

Karlsson, Bengt. 2003. 'Anthropology and the 'Indigenous Slot': Claims to and Debates about Indigenous Peoples' Status in India.' *Critique of Anthropology* 23(4): 403–23.

Katan, David. 'Defining Culture, Defining Translation.' In *The Routledge Handbook of Translation and Culture*, edited by Sue-Ann Harding and Ovidi Carbonell Cortes, 17–47. London: Routledge.

Kolnai, Aurel. 1976. 'Dignity.' *Philosophy* 51(197): 251–71.

Kumar, Sujit. 2014. 'Interrogating 'Integration' in Adivasi Discourse.' *Journal of Adivasi and Indigenous Studies* 1(1): 62–75.

Kundu, Abhijit. et al. 2005. *The Humanities: Methodology and Perspectives*. New Delhi: Pearson Education.

Latour, Bruno. 2005. *Reassembling the Social: An Introduction to Actor-Network-Theory*. Oxford: Oxford University Press.

Luis, Sandip. 2019. 'Between Anthropology and History: The Entangled Lives of Jangarh Singh Shyam and Jagdish Swaminathan.' In *Intersections of Contemporary Art, Anthropology and Art History in South Asia*, 139–79. Cham: Palgrave Macmillan.

Macdougall, John. 1977. 'Agrarian reforms vs. religious revitalisation: collective resistance to peasantization among the Mundas, Oraons and Santals, 1858–95.' *Contributions to Indian Sociology* 11(2): 295–327.

Mahato, Pashupati Prasad. 1987. *The Performing Arts of Jharkhand*. Calcutta: B.B. Prakashan.

Mahato, Pashupati Prasad. 1997. 'The Status of the Kudmi-Mahatos in the Hor-Mitan and Hor-Diku Dichotomy: A Study of Ethno-history and Inter-ethnic Relations in Jharkhand.' *Social Change* 27: 1–2.

Mahato, Pashupati Prasad. 2000. *Sanskritization vs Nirbakization: A Study of Cultural Silence and Ethnic Memocide in Jharkhand.* Kolkata: Sujan Publications.

Mahato, Pashupati Prasad. 2003. 'Changing World Views of the Indigenous (Mulvasi-Adivasi) People of Jharkhand: A Socio-Philosophical Perspective.' In *Changing Tribal Life: A Socio-philosophical Perspective*, edited by Padmaja Sen, 50–61. New Delhi: Concept Publishing.

Maitland, Sarah. 2017. *What is Cultural Translation?* London: Bloomsbury.

Mandal, Dilip. 2021. 'Shudra Identity and Struggle: A Trans-Temporal Journey from the Rigveda to the Constitution.' *Economic and Political Weekly* 23 October LVI(43): 24–25.

Marglin, S. 1990. *Dominating Knowledge: Development, Culture, and Resistance.* Oxford: Clarendon Press.

Mattson, David and Susan Clark. 2011. 'Human dignity in concept and practice.' *Policy Science* 44: 303–19.

McKeon, Richard. 1957. 'Responsibility as Sign and Instrumentality', Unpublished paper, Richard Peter McKeon Papers, University of Chicago Library Archives, Series 3: 127.

McKeon, Richard. 1957a. 'The Development and the Significance of the Concept of Responsibility.' *Revue Internationale de Philosophie* 11(39): 3–32.

McKeon, Richard. 1959. 'Principles and Consequences.' *The Journal of Philosophy* 56(9): 385–401.

McKeon, Richard. 1960. 'Being, Existence, and That Which Is.' *The Review of Metaphysics* 13(4): 539–54.

McKeon, Richard, 1964. 'Mankind: Relation of Reason to Action.' *Ethics* 74(3): 174–85.

McKeon, Richard. 1968. 'Philosophy and History in the Development of Human Rights.' In *Ethics and Social Justice*, edited by Howard Kiefer and Milton Munitz, 300–22. Albany: State University of New York Press.

McKeon, Richard, 1970. 'Concluding Remarks on Metaphysics, Politics and Contemporary Unrest.' *Metaphilosophy* 1(1): 85–90.

McKeon, Richard. 1978. 'Person and Community: Metaphysical and Political.' *Ethics* 88(3): 207–217.

Medves, Zdenko. 2019. 'Education for Values.' In *New Pedagogical Challenges in the 21st Century: Contributions of Research in Education*, edited by Olga Cavero and Nuria Llevot-Calvet, 73–96. London: IntechOpen.

Meijers, Frans and Hubert Hermans. 2017. 'Dialogical Self Theory in Education: An Introduction.' In *The Dialogical Self Theory in Education: A Multicultural Perspective*, edited by Frans Meijers and Hubert Hermans, 1–19. Cham: Springer International Publishing.

Mersmann, Birgit and Hans Kippenberg, eds. 2016. *The Humanities between Global Integration and Cultural Diversity*. Berlin: De Gruyter.

Mignolo, Walter. 2006. 'Citizenship, Knowledge, and the Limits of History.' *American Literary History* 18(2): 323–31.

Mignolo, Walter. 2021. *The politics of decolonial investigations*. Durham: Duke University Press.

Miri, Mrinal. 2014. *Philosophy and Education*. New Delhi: Oxford University Press.

Miri, Mrinal, ed. 2017. *The Place of Humanities in Our Universities*. Abingdon: Routledge.

Mitra, Santanu and Ganga Nath Jha. 2015. 'Santal Bongas.' *Journal of the Anthropological Survey of India* 64(1–2): 47–58.

Mohanty, Ranjita and Rajesh Tandon, eds. 2006. *Participatory Citizenship: Identity, Exclusion, Inclusion*. New Delhi: Sage.

Morreira, Shannon, et al, eds. 2021. *Decolonising Curricula and Pedagogy in Higher Education*. Abingdon: Routledge.

Muller Mirza, Nathalie and Marcelo Dos Santos Mamed. 2021. 'A Dialogical Approach to Dialogue in Learning.' In *Dialogical Approaches and Tensions in Learning and Development: At the Frontiers of Mind*, edited by Nathalie Muller Mirza and Marcelo Dos Santos Mamed, 1–12. Cham: Springer.

Munda, Jaipal Singh. 1939. 'Adibasi Sabha Deputation.' *The Bihar Herald* 11 July: 16.

Murmu, Suresh Chandra and Nilamadhaba Kanhar. 2014. 'Santal Durbar and its Democratic Role.' *Adivasi* 54(1–2): 83–91.

Nair, Rukmini Bhaya et al. 2019. 'Grand Challenges for the Humanities in India.' Report submitted to the Ministry for Human Resource Development.

Nascimento, Amos and Matthias Lutz-Bachmann, eds. 2017. *Human Dignity: Perspectives from a Critical Theory of Human Rights*. Abingdon: Routledge.

National Gallery of Modern Art. 2021. *Bapu* (Virtual Exhibition), ngmaindia.gov.in/virtual-tour-of-bapu.asp.

Niezen, Ronald. 2003. *The Origins of Indigenism: Human Rights and the Politics of Identity*. Berkeley: University of California Press.

Nilsen, Alf. 2019. *Adivasis and the State: Subalternity and Citizenship in India's Bhil Heartland*. Cambridge: Cambridge University Press.

Nussbaum, Martha. 1997. *Cultivating Humanity: A Classical Defence of Reform in Liberal Education*. Cambridge, Massachusetts: Harvard University Press.

Pankaj, Ashwini Kumar ed. 2017. *Adivasidom: Selected Writing and Speeches of Jaipal Singh Munda*. Ranchi: Pyara Kerketta Foundation.

Panikkar, K. N. and M. Bhaskaran Nair, eds. 2011. *Emerging Trends in Higher Education in India: Concepts and Practices*. Delhi: Longman.

Panthaki, Neville G. 2016. *Conceptualizing the State-Nation via Education Reform: from Multicultural to Intercultural Citizenship* (PhD Dissertation). Toronto: Ontario Institute for Studies in Education.

Peet, Richard and Elaine Hartwick. 2015. *Theories of Development: Contentions, Arguments, Alternatives*. New York: The Guildford Press.

Pfeffer, Georg, and Deepak Kumar Behera. 1997. *Contemporary Society: Concept of Tribal Society*. New Delhi: Concept Publishing.

Phillips, Ruth. 2021. '"Changing up" the museum: cultural translation and decolonial politics', *ICOFOM Study Series* 49(2): 196–212.

Plummer, Ken. 2021. *Critical Humanism: A Manifesto for the 21st Century*. Cambridge: Polity Press.

Rao, Nitya. 2005. 'Displacement from Land: Case of Santhal Parganas.' *Economic and Political Weekly* 40(41): 4439–42.

Rao, V. Srinivasa, ed. 2019. *Adivasi Rights and Exclusion in India*. Abingdon: Routledge.

Restreop, Eduardo. 2018. 'World Anthropologies', *The International Encyclopaedia of Anthropology*, John Wiley and Sons. https://onlinelibrary.wiley.com/doi/10.1002/9781118924396.wbiea2119.

Robin, Cyril. 2009. 'Jharkhand: Between Tribal Mobilisation and the Rise of the OBC.' In *Rise of the Plebians?*, edited by Christophe Jaffrelot and Sanjay Kumar, 313–325. New Delhi: Routledge.

Rycroft, Daniel. 1996. 'Born from the Soil: the Indigenous Mural Aesthetic of Kheroals in Jharkhand, eastern India.' *South Asian Studies* 12: 67–81.

Rycroft, Daniel (dir.). 2005. 'Hul Sengel: The Spirit of the Santal Revolution.' New Delhi: ICITP in association with the University of Sussex.

Rycroft, Daniel. 2006. *Representing Rebellion: The Visual Aspects of Counter-insurgency in Colonial India*. New Delhi: Oxford University Press.

Rycroft, Daniel. 2006a. 'Santalism: Reconfiguring 'the Santal' in Indian art and politics.' *Indian Historical Review* 33(1): 150–74.

Rycroft, Daniel. 2011. 'Beyond Resistance: Idioms and Memories of Insurgency in the Adivasi Movement in Jharkhand.' In *Narratives from the Margins: Aspects of Adivasi History in India*, edited by Sanjukta Dasgupta and R.S. Basu, 257–76. New Delhi: Primus Books.

Rycroft, Daniel. 2011a. 'After-Images: Visual Cultures and Subaltern Pasts.' *Visual Culture in Britain* 12(3): 367–86.

Rycroft, Daniel. 2012. 'Indian Anthropology and the Construction of 'Tribal Ethnicity' before Independence.' In *Nationhood and Identity Movements in Asia: Colonial and Postcolonial Times*, edited by Swarupa Gupta, 141–65. New Delhi: Manohar Publishers.

Rycroft, Daniel. 2012a. 'From History to Heritage: Adivasi Identity and Hul Sengel.' In *Voices from the Periphery: Subalternity and Empowerment in India*, edited by Marine Carrin and Lidia Guzy, 48–74. New Delhi: Routledge.

Rycroft, Daniel. 2012b. 'India's Adivasis (Indigenous/Tribal Peoples) and Anthropological Heritage.' In *Anthropologists, Indigenous Scholars and the Research Endeavour: Seeking Bridges Towards Mutual Respect*, edited by Joy Hendry and Laara Fitznoor, 80–93. New York: Routledge.

Rycroft, Daniel. 2013. 'Co-existence and Art Historical Apprehensions.' In *World Art and the Legacies of Colonial Violence*, edited by Daniel Rycroft, 231–51. Farnham: Ashgate.

Rycroft, Daniel. 2014. 'Reinterpreting Adivasi History: Memory of the Santal Revolution in Village Bhognadih.' In *Dissent, Discrimination and Dispossession: Tribal Movements in Contemporary India*, edited by K. Misra and N.K. Das, 51–71. New Delhi: Manohar Publishers.

Rycroft, Daniel. 2014a. 'Looking beyond the present: The Historical Dynamics of Adivasi (Indigenous and tribal) Assertions in India (Part 1).' *Journal of Adivasi and Indigenous Studies* 1(1): 1–17.

Rycroft, Daniel. 2014b. 'Historical Anthropology and 'The Primitive': Rethinking the 1931 Census of India.' In *The Politics of Ethnicity in India, Nepal and China*, edited by Marine Carrin et al, 25–54. Delhi: Primus Books.

Rycroft, Daniel. 2015. 'Looking Beyond the Present: The Historical Dynamics of Adivasi (Indigenous and Tribal) Assertions in India (Part 2).' *Journal of Adivasi and Indigenous Studies* 2(1): 1–10.

Rycroft, Daniel. 2015a. 'Locating Adivasi Politics: Aspects of 'Indian' Anthropology after Birsa Munda.' *Anglistica* 19(1): 133–46.

Rycroft, Daniel. 2016. 'Anthropological archives and 'chiasmic' time in modern India.' *Irish Journal of Anthropology* 16(2): 46–68.

Rycroft, Daniel. 2017. 'Anthropology as Satyagraha (Truth-force): Elwin in pre-independence India.' In *Pathways of Creative Research: Towards a Festival of Dialogues*, edited by Ananta Kumar Giri, 9–30. New Delhi: Primus Books.

Rycroft, Daniel. 2017a. 'Adivasi Worlds: Encountering 'Indian' idealism in anthropology before independence.' In *Environment and the Adivasi World*, edited by Mahua Sarkar, 29–58. Kolkata: Alphabet Books.

Rycroft, Daniel and Ganesh Devy. 2014. 'Dialogue on Indigenous Studies and Fieldwork in India.' In *Fieldwork in South Asia: Memories, Moments, and Experiences*, edited by Sarit Chaudhuri and Sucheta Sen Chaudhuri, 339–60. New Delhi: Sage Publications.

Rycroft, Daniel, ed. 2021. *Dialogues on Decolonisation*, Norwich: UEA (India Dialogue).

Rycroft, Daniel and Sangeeta Dasgupta, eds. 2011. *The Politics of Belonging in India: Becoming Adivasi*. Abingdon: Routledge.

Rycroft, Daniel et al, eds. 2020. *University Social Responsibility: From Dialogue to Implementation*. Norwich: UEA (India Dialogue).

Schroeder, Heike. 2020. 'What Role for Indigenous Knowledge and Emotional Literacy in Implementing the SDGs?' In *University Social Responsibility: From Dialogue to Implementation*, edited by Daniel Rycroft, et al 28–29. Norwich: UEA (India Dialogue).

Shrinkhal, Rashweet. 2017. 'Tribes as 'Indigenous Peoples': Revisiting Indigeneity Debate in India.' *The Oriental Anthropologist* 17(2): 213–35.

Singh, Anoop K. 2013. 'Defying the Odds: The Triumphs and Tragedies of Dalit and Adivasi Students in Higher Education.' In *Beyond Inclusion: The Practices of Equal Access in Indian Higher Education*, edited by Satish Deshpande and Usma Zacharias, 174–204. London: Routledge.

Sinha, Surajit. 1965. 'Tribe-Case and Tribe-Peasant Continua in Central India.' *Man in India* 45(1): 57–83.

Somanboina, Simhadri and Akhileshwari Ramagoud, eds. 2022. *The Routledge Handbook of the Other Backward Classes in India: Thought, Movements and Development*. Abingdon: Routledge.

Sondhi, G. C. 1940. 'Birsa Bhagwan: Rebel Prophet of Adibasis.' In *Congress Souvenir Ramgarh*, edited by G. C. Sondhi, 88–90. Calcutta: The Commercial Syndicate.

Sondhi, G. C., ed. 1948. *To the Gates of Liberty* (Congress Commemoration Volume). Calcutta: Swadesh Bharati.

Spiegelberg, Herbert. 1971. 'Human Dignity: A Challenge to Contemporary Philosophy.' *The Philosophy Forum* 9: 39–64.

Sustainable Development Solutions Network. 2017. *Getting Started with the SDGs in Universities: A Guide for Universities, Higher Education Institutions, and the Academic Sector*. Melbourne: SDSN.

Thapar, Romesh, et al. 1970. 'Towards a new value system.' In *Cultural Rights as Human Rights*, edited by UNESCO, 89–104. Paris: UNESCO.

United Nations. 2014. *The Road to Dignity by 2030* (Synthesis Report of the Secretary-General on the Post-2015 Agenda). New York: United Nations.

UNESCO, ed. 1999. *Towards a Constructive Pluralism*. Paris: UNESCO.

UNESCO Editorial. 2017. 'Agenda 2030: UNESCO and the SDGs.' *The UNESCO Courier* (April–June): 7.

Upadhyay, Vijay and Gaya Pandey. 1993. *History of Anthropological Thought*. New Delhi: Concept Publishing.

Vasudevan, Hari. 2018. 'Challenges of Curriculum Development', University of Calcutta and University of East Anglia Roundtable, 2 February, Kolkata.

Vazquez, Rolando. 2021. *Vistas of Modernity: Decolonial Aesthetics and the End of the Contemporary*. Brouwersgracht: Mondriaan Fund.

Vveinhardt, Jolita, ed. 2017. *Congruence of Personal and Organizational Values*. Rijeka: InTech.

Wane, Njoki and Kimberly Todd. 2018. 'Introduction: A Meeting of Decolonial Minds.' In *Decolonial Pedagogy: Examining Sites of Resistance, Resurgence, and Renewal*, edited by Njoki Wane and Kimberly Todd, 1–8. Cham: Palgrave Macmillan.

Weber, H. 2017. 'Politics of 'Leaving No One Behind': Contesting the 2030 Sustainable Development Goals Agenda.' *Globalizations* 14(3): 399–414.

Weber, Luc. 2012. 'The responsibility of universities to promote a sustainable society.' In *Global Sustainability and the Responsibility of Universities*, edited by Luc Weber and James Duderstadt, 229–50. Washington, DC: Brookings Institution Press.

White, Stephen. 2007. 'Aurobindo's Thought and Holistic Global Education.' *Journal of Thought* (Fall–Winter): 115–32.

Wilson, Richard. 1991. 'Reconciling Universalism and Relativism in Political Culture: A View Based on Economic and Psychological Perspectives.' *Journal of Asian Studies* 50(1): 53–66.

Xaxa, Virginius. 2016. 'The Global Indigenous Peoples Movement: It's Stirring in India.' *Journal of Law, Property and Society* 2: 141–60.

Yap, M. Li-Ming and K. Watene. 2019. 'The Sustainable Development Goals (SDGs) and Indigenous Peoples: Another Missed Opportunity?' *Journal of Human Development and Capabilities* 20(4): 451–67.